THE REVENANT

30 DEVOTIONS
from ACTS *to*
BREATHE LIFE
into the
CHURCH

CHRISTIAN CHAPMAN

ILLUMIFY
MEDIA.COM

The Revenant
Copyright © 2024 by Christian Chapman

All rights reserved. No part of this book may be reproduced in any form or by any means—whether electronic, digital, mechanical, or otherwise—without permission in writing from the publisher, except by a reviewer, who may quote brief passages in a review.

Unless otherwise noted, all Scripture is from The Holy Bible, English Standard Version. ESV® Text Edition: 2016. Copyright © 2001 by Crossway Bibles, a publishing ministry of Good News Publishers. Scripture marked NASB is from the New American Standard Bible®, Copyright © 1960, 1971, 1977, 1995, 2020 by The Lockman Foundation. All rights reserved. Scripture marked NIV is from the Holy Bible, New International Version®, NIV® Copyright ©1973, 1978, 1984, 2011 by Biblica, Inc.® Used by permission. All rights reserved worldwide. Scripture marked NLT is from the *Holy Bible*, New Living Translation, copyright © 1996, 2004, 2015 by Tyndale House Foundation. Used by permission of Tyndale House Publishers, Inc., Carol Stream, Illinois 60188. All rights reserved. Scripture marked NKJV is taken from the New King James Version®. Copyright © 1982 by Thomas Nelson. Used by permission. All rights reserved.

The views and opinions expressed in this book are those of the author and do not necessarily reflect the official policy or position of Illumify Media Global.

Published by
Illumify Media Global
www.IllumifyMedia.com
"Let's bring your book to life!"

Paperback ISBN: 978-1-964251-17-2

Cover design by Debbie Lewis

Printed in the United States of America

Contents

Thank You	v
Day 1: Introduction	1
Day 2: Alive and Well	5
Day 3: COVID (<u>C</u>hurch <u>O</u>n <u>V</u>ision <u>I</u>ntensive <u>D</u>ebacle)	13
Day 4: Gold, Silver, and Things that Shine	21
Day 5: What Burns Within?	30
Day 6: A Faith That Gives Life	37
Day 7: Answer the Call Before the Fall	45
Day 8: Small Things Made Great	52
Day 9: Not For Nothing	61
Day 10: In the Blink of an Eye	70
Day 11: Wall Destroyers	77
Day 12: It's Not About Me, But We	85
Day 13: Peace by Prayer	93
Day 14: To Be Called Christian	100
Day 15: Pride's Antidote	107
Day 16: The Majors and Minors of Faith	114
Day 17: Stops and Steps	122
Day 18: Wows and Woahs	129
Day 19: Prep Rallies	137
Day 20: Who Knows Your Name?	145
Day 21: Lights, Camera, ~~Action~~ Tears!	153
Day 22: Following His Lead	164
Day 23: He Uses Us	171

Day 24: Sands of Providence	178
Day 25: The Killer of Tens of Thousands	185
Day 26: Perils of Placating	192
Day 27: Freedom in Chains	200
Day 28: Drop the Anchor	207
Day 29: No Scar?	216
Day 30: Angels in the Cracks	224

Thank You

There are so many people to thank in helping me accomplish this project, but the most important thank you I have to recognize goes to my Lord and Savior Jesus Christ. His death for me on the cross gives me the ability to live a life of hope and share His message of love with those in need of the gospel. I love you, Lord!

Pastor Kelvin Smith, lead pastor of Steele Creek Church of Charlotte, and all those in the body of Christ there which I still call family, thank you. You have helped me complete this project with your financial and prayerful support and I can't thank you enough. No matter where the Holy Spirit takes me, I will always consider Steele Creek Church of Charlotte my home church and Pastor Kelvin the best mentor a brother could have. I love you!

Tom and Gloria Kasler, who befriended me when I first moved to Bluffton, South Carolina, you both inspired me daily to stay the course and persevere during times when my spirit was low. Your financial support for this project and your faithful encouragement to me is one of the bricks in the foundation of *The Revenant*. Thank you for continuing to love me, keep up with me, and pray for me as I passionately follow the Holy Spirit's calling in my life. I love you!

Paul Schmidt, who is a faithful member at New Life Church where I currently pastor, you have personally given financial blessing to help finish the final chapters of this project when all of the resources had run out. I also thank you for all the times you have taken me to lunch just to encourage me and keep my spirits lifted so I could finish the race the Holy Spirit called me to run. My brother, enjoy your retirement and know that I love you!

The Twin Harbor Worship Center in Lake Tillery, North Carolina, who has a deep love for the ancient church and expresses it in their current house of worship, has been a huge financial support. They feel, as I do, that the book of Acts and the birth of the early church is a powerful message to get out to our modern churches in today's culture. I thank my brothers and sisters, and I love you!

I would like to thank my very talented ghostwriter, Rebecca Lindsey, who has done an incredible job of helping the pages of the book of Acts and the early church come to life. It has been a joy to work with you, my sister. I can't wait to see what project God opens up for you next. Just know that I pray for you, and I'm believing in big things for your life. I love you!

Last, but certainly not least, is New Life Church, my current church family where I have been called to serve in Bluffton, South Carolina as lead pastor. We have been through difficult changes and challenges, but through it all, we have continued to love and support one another. I cannot thank you enough. You have encouraged and supported me as I have walked through the Alzheimer's journey with my mom and lifted my spirits at times when I needed it the most. I look forward to what God has for us in the low country of South Carolina and beyond. I could not love you enough!

Grace and peace,
Pastor Christian Chapman

Introduction

Day 1

In 2015, an incredible movie came out called *The Revenant*. It was based on the true story of Hugh Glass, a frontiersman in the 1800s who was on a fur expedition with other trackers in the wilderness when he wandered upon a black bear. Almost immediately, the bear viciously mauls him, biting and ripping his flesh. Because of the severity of his wounds and the distance the other trackers would have to carry him for medical attention, they decided to leave him for dead. Little did they know, Glass wouldn't die, but instead would tend to his own wounds. He used maggots to eat away the infection and even set his own broken leg. Amazingly, he found the strength to crawl his way back to civilization. This resourceful tracker traveled two hundred miles in six weeks, surviving on berries and plant roots while taking the full brunt of Mother Nature's vengeance. You see, *The Revenant* is a movie about a man's desire to live when everyone else believed he was dead and not worth fighting for. For me, this book is the same.

In my thirty years of ministry experience, I'd be lying if I said I didn't see similar struggles, suffering, and death within aspects of the church today. A place that's ordinarily filled with beauty and purpose is more commonly filled with complacent hearts and dry spiritual tanks. All of the beauty that should be—the strangers who make us feel like family, the friends who hold our hands when we're down and out, the counselors who help us find our way to a purpose-driven life—is too often mortally wounded and left for dead in the wilderness.

However, we both know that the church was never meant to be this way. There is so much beauty in the church. Beauty worth fighting for. It truly is a place where people are reborn and come back to life. Across all denominations, the church is a place where the message of Jesus Christ is lifted up and communicated with love.

How badly I want that beauty to be evident at all times, in all churches, throughout all denominations. Which is why in the midst of the death and complacency the modern church is facing, I write to you.

You! Perhaps the person who not only sees the same fractured pieces of the church but feels them in your own heart. This book is all about rediscovering the church's beauty and seeing what was once dead come back to life. This way, we can be an effective church that pleases the Lord. The truth is that the bride is full of potential, but we need to make sure she is seeking out the right groom.

With many different religions rejecting Christ and more than thirty thousand churches within the Protestant faith ignoring Scripture to fulfill a more comfortable personal agenda, it's important to understand who we're called to be and what we're called to do. In times like these, we must look to the early church for answers. This blueprint for beauty can be found in the book of Acts, where the early church was born.

As you venture through these pages, you will rediscover what was lost in order to help others discover the gospel of Christ in Spirit and in truth. Yes, I deeply believe God wants to do a new

Day 1: Introduction

thing in your heart and in the heart of the church. But as it turns out, this new thing God wants to do will come from old biblical principles that have never lost their power or relevancy. God has promised the church beautiful success in our call to do kingdom work. I believe we can accomplish this work by looking back and remembering the early church and where we came from.

So, as we journey ahead, I pray that you have an open heart to what the Spirit of God might say and do in your life through this experience. It doesn't matter if you're a famous heart surgeon or a sick patient under his or her scalpel. It doesn't matter if you're a mighty shepherd standing on a hill with staff in hand or a defenseless sheep grazing cautiously in the valley below. It isn't important if you're an Ivy League professor or a freshman student who still can't find the cafeteria on campus. It doesn't mean a thing if you're a wealthy entrepreneur with bank accounts in multiple countries or an out-of-work widow with three kids and no money in her one account.

No matter who you are or where you come from, I truly believe there is an awakening that will take place if you have ears to hear. You might ask, "Why do I need ears when I'm going to read your book?" By committing to reading *The Revenant*, studying the history of the early church, and learning what it has to do with you, I believe the Holy Spirit will whisper to your heart. That whisper is what will make the greatest change in your life commitment to the church. It's what will make you into a warrior for the gospel, reviving what once was dead and bringing it back to life.

Without a doubt, it's a thin line we will have to walk to get to where we are going. But with a commitment to learning God's direction for the church and watering each day with prayer, I believe *The Revenant* will bring you back to life.

The Revenant

In *The Revenant,* I have written thirty daily readings based on the book of Acts—with each day coinciding with a chapter. While Acts has twenty-eight chapters (hence, twenty-eight daily readings), I have included a twenty-ninth chapter that concludes our time together. Technically speaking, please consider this your first daily reading.

Buckle up, stand strong, and get ready. I can't wait to see what the Lord is going to do.

Alive and Well

Day 2

"Our Lord has written the promise of resurrection, not only in books alone, but in every leaf in springtime."
Martin Luther

"He presented himself alive to them after his suffering by many proofs, appearing to them during forty days and speaking about the kingdom of God."

Acts 1:3

I love springtime. Probably because the sights and sounds of God's creation come back to life. Trees once abandoned by dying leaves spring back to life in a colorful display. Mountains once filled with snow begin to melt and give way to a kaleidoscope of color as wildflowers begin to bloom. Birds once dormant come out to sing a song of celebration as a new season of life begins.

Springtime has a way of waking all of creation.

And if all these examples could sing one chorus together, it would certainly be "Alive and Well."

That is the epitome of what God does to us, after all. He takes the broken and dead parts of our souls and revives them. With his glory and power, he makes us alive and well in the Spirit.

God chooses to physically and spiritually revive several people in the Bible. The apostle Paul was one of them. We read about his "alive and well" moments in his letter to the church of Corinth.

> Five times I received at the hand of the Jews the forty lashes less one. Three times I was beaten with rods. Once I was stoned. Three times I was shipwrecked; a night and a day I was adrift at sea; on frequent journeys . . . And, apart from all other things, there is the daily pressure on me of my anxiety for all the churches. (2 Corinthians 11:24-26, 28, ESV)

If this were a Psalm being sung from Paul's heart, it would certainly be called Alive and Well. How do you stop a man like that? Can you imagine the frustration of the Enemy who tried to silence this man's voice for the gospel? Their conversation might have sounded something like this:

The Enemy: We're going to kill you.
Paul: To die is gain.
The Enemy: Okay, we will leave you alone.
Paul: To live is Christ.
The Enemy: Well, we will torture you.
Paul: Go ahead. I don't compare the sufferings of this world to be compared to future glory.
The Enemy: Well, then we will throw you in prison.
Paul: Then send down a hymnal, because I'm going to sing praise songs to God and convert all your guards.

Not even torture or death threatened to stop Paul from living for Christ. And how was this possible? Because Paul's righteousness was a foreign righteousness—one that is not from this world. And for what purpose? To share the message of Christ with a lost world.

In the Gospel of Luke, we see the story of a prodigal son who squanders his father's inheritance on wild living (chapter 15). Eventually, he comes to his senses and heads back home to ask for forgiveness. When his father sees him, the celebration begins.

This father was certainly alive and well in his love. How was this possible? Because of a foreign love. For what purpose? So the world would know the love of the heavenly Father.

How about the thief on the cross who repented to Jesus before his death? We read his final moments in the Gospel of Luke.

> One of the criminals who were hanged railed at him, saying, "Are you not the Christ? Save yourself and us!" But the other rebuked him, saying, "Do you not fear God, since you are under the same sentence of condemnation? And we indeed justly, for what we are receiving the due rewards for our deeds; but this man has done nothing wrong." And he said, "Jesus, remember me when you come into your kingdom." And he said to him, "Truly I say to you, today you will be with me in paradise" (Luke 23:39-43).

How was this possible? Because of a foreign grace. For what purpose? So the world would know the blood of Christ washes away every stain from every vein. All of these "alive and well" moments occur for one specific purpose: to give God the glory.

The Work of Waiting

Years ago, I had an "alive and well" moment when I was traveling as an itinerant speaker. It was a moment I will never forget. I was just starting my full-time call to evangelistic ministries and accepted a position with Kingdom Building Ministries (KBM) out of Aurora, Colorado. It's safe to say that the beginning stages of my newfound calling to evangelism got off to a slow start because of the way KBM believed the Holy Spirit works in an evangelist's life. From day one, I was told that they were not going to advertise my ministry or put me ahead of other speakers because if it was God's calling for me to speak, how could it be stopped?

Jesus knows that it's hard to make a difference unless you have a foreign presence living inside you. And this chapter of Acts reminds us of the important work of simply waiting for God to live in us—waiting for Him to stir in us, so we can do His will.

That's exactly what I did. For my first year speaking, I waited on The Lord. I trusted the call He had put on my heart. If no one called asking for Christian Chapman, then it wasn't what God wanted, and I would pray for my plans to line up with His.

As I look back on this extreme time of uncertainty and fear, I see now how great a lesson it was to trust God's voice in my life. What KBM was trying to teach me was that when God calls, heaven falls. And the gates of hell cannot prevail against it.

And with that, the first call came in.

I was requested by Fayetteville Christian School in North Carolina to be a special guest speaker for their chapel service. This was my first big chance to pursue the calling God spoke into my heart. You can bet I was prayed up, praised up, prepped up, and ready to preach up.

Moments before I walked on stage for my very first speaking opportunity, the Holy Spirit started talking. And He wasn't saying something easy either. In fact, He told me *not* to speak but to give an altar call.

I began frantically debating God.

Day 2: Alive And Well

What about my prep time in the Word? And the sermon I was prepared to preach? I began questioning His judgment and understanding of the situation. *If I obey you, will I blow my one speaking opportunity at this school? Will they ever invite me back?*

But in His goodness, God took the responsibility off me and put it on Him. He reminded me that the students were ready to get saved not because of anything I had prepared but because of what He would do through me. So with my questions and uncertainty, I raised my head and decided to obey.

To this day, I don't know why I said what I did. It wasn't in my notes nor was it something God had recently challenged me to preach on. Regardless, it was the first thing that came out of my mouth: "Muhammad and Gandhi and all other gods are dead and buried. But our Savior, Jesus Christ, has risen from the grave! His tomb is still empty today, inviting everyone inside to see that death and hell have been defeated."

That was it.

That was the depth and length of the sermon I drove over two hours to preach. And it was more than enough.

How was this possible? Because it was foreign and not of this world. For what purpose? To bring many to know God's great name.

This "alive and well" moment moved waves of kids to the altar until it was full. Then the second and third rows at the front were full. And then the floor of the gymnasium was full of a sea of students weeping and collapsing and praising and singing. Only God could have filled that altar that day in that way. Sure, I could have preached and emotionally stirred a few hearts, but that kind of altar call required a deeper presence—a foreign presence. Can it get any better? It did!

Later that week, I received a call from the principal informing me that one of her exchange students from the Middle East had complained about my comments on Muhammed still being in the grave and how Jesus was alive and well. She encouraged her to process my comments and ask God to reveal the truth of them to her heart.

And so, she did. And so, He did.

About three months later, another KBM speaker went to the same school to preach in the same chapel. Without knowing what happened last time, he also did an altar call, unknowingly repeating my exact words about Muhammad being in the grave and Jesus being alive and well. That's when the young exchange student from the Middle East boldly walked to the altar and gave her life to Christ. Not only that, but she was already leading the other exchange students from her country to Christ as well.

A complete revival was taking place at Fayetteville Christian School. Through this "alive and well" story, I was learning it was not about me, my flesh, or my worldly resources to revive the hearts of people. But only the power of God that lives inside of me. He presented himself alive to me, just like He did to the disciples!

How the Church Can Let Go to Become Alive

It takes a foreign presence from heaven to empower the journey for earthly kingdom work to be fulfilled. Hold on to that thought as we bring in one more resurrection story to help drive home our revenant moment from the chapter. It's the story of Lazarus:

> Now a certain man was ill, Lazarus of Bethany . . . so the sisters sent to him, saying, "Lord, he whom you love is ill," But when

Day 2: Alive And Well

Jesus had heard it he said, "This illness does not lead to death. It is for the glory of God, so that the Son of God may be glorified through it." (John 11:1-6, ESV)

Out of frustration with Jesus' lack of haste, Mary and Martha reminded Jesus that Lazarus was ill. The obvious questions that Martha and Mary probably wanted to ask: Why would Jesus stay two more days when He knew Lazarus was deathly ill? Why wouldn't He just heal him now? I believe the answer to this question is found in Jesus' response to Martha:

> I am the resurrection and the life. Whoever believes in me, though he die, yet shall he live, and everyone who lives and believes in me shall never die. Do you believe this?" She said to him, "Yes, Lord. I believe." (John 11:25-27, ESV)

The reason for his waiting was for her growth. The reason He delayed was to glorify God and provide us with "alive and well" faith moments.

Mary and Martha were concerned about the wrong thing. Similarly, I believe this is the state of the church today. I believe God is waiting for us, like He was for Mary and Martha, to stop chasing a worldly plan in accomplishing a worldly ministry. We must stop supporting seed-planting preachers who fly on private planes and ride in luxury cars when Paul made tents to take the pressure off the church and provide the gospel for free.

We must realize that being alive and well comes only from a foreign presence that can't be found in anything that feeds the flesh. Peter declares, "Beloved, I urge you as aliens and strangers to abstain from fleshly lusts which wage war against your soul" (1 Peter 2:11, NASB).

The truth is we will always struggle to bring what pleases the flesh into our way of worship, but what truly revives us has nothing to do with this world. You see, the revenant is all about the dead coming back to life. To be alive and well doesn't require anything from the world, since the world can only offer happiness, which is temporary. But joy? Joy is everlasting. It will fill our hearts and sustain us for longer than a season, instead for all eternity.

COVID (<u>C</u>hurch <u>O</u>n <u>V</u>ision <u>I</u>ntensive <u>D</u>ebacle)

ᴅ)ᴀʏ 3

"Vision without action is merely a dream. Action without vision just passes the time. Vision with action can change the world."
Joel Barker

"And they devoted themselves to the apostles' teaching and the fellowship, to the breaking of bread and the prayers."

Acts 2:42

I wasn't raised in a church where people threw their hands in the air when worshiping or spoke in tongues when the Spirit came over them. No one danced in celebration of the Christian life or shouted, *"Amen!"* enthusiastically from the pews. I grew up to understand that good Weslyans just don't do that.

There were lots of things we *did* do, however. At the church where I was born and raised, First Wesleyan Church, we started right at 11 a.m. and ended right at 12 p.m. Ours was a church where old hymns were sung, and the Bible was preached. Men wore ties and women wore long dresses. The pastor stood at the door after each service, personally shaking people's hands and proclaiming blessings over their upcoming week.

But like I said, some things we just didn't do, like speaking prophetic dreams.

Well, that is, until God gave me a certain prophetic dream just before the coronavirus hit our shores in 2020.

In this dream from God, I was walking through the streets of a large city where sin had completely taken over. Drugs were openly being sold. Prostitution was celebrated and found on every corner. Theft and murder were rampant. The homeless population was at an all-time high. I began to experience the same feeling of hopelessness Jonah must have felt while walking the streets of Nineveh. As I carried my Bible through crowds of people, I began to empathize with Lot while living in Sodom and Gomorrah. At first, people were listening. Some were even responding. But in the dream, it became obvious that while the harvest was plentiful, the workers were few. That's when I began to look for help.

In the midst of all the crime and hopelessness in my dream, there also happened to be churches on every corner. This seemed strange to me, considering there was no one from the church on the streets. If there was such a need for the good news of Jesus to be heard, where were all the Christians? Why weren't they on these streets sharing?

Well, I assumed they were meeting and perhaps not aware of the need. With an eager hope to spread the gospel, I ran into each church, desperately trying to recruit Christians to fulfill Romans 10:14-15:

> How then will they call on him in whom they have not believed? And how are they to believe in him whom they have never heard? And how are they to hear without someone preaching? And how

Day 3: Covid (church On Vision Intensive Debacle)

are they to preach unless they are sent? . . . How beautiful are the feet of those who preach the good news!

My legs grew tired from running from church to church, each one turning out to be empty.

Typically in my dreams, the only senses I recall the next morning are what I saw and heard. Never have I experienced a dream so vividly that I experienced all my senses. As I continued to search each church for any signs of life, this horrifying stench came over me. No matter the church I entered, the awful odor continued to fill the air. As I ran and spoke, I felt my mouth getting dry from passionately sharing the gospel to deaf ears. The noise of the chaos and celebration of sin rang through the streets from all around the city. It was all too much. The heaviness of the attack of the Enemy on God's creation weighed on my heart and body. I felt like passing out.

But I knew what I needed to do. I needed to spread the gospel all over the city and recruit other believers. In my agony, I ignored the stench for as long as I could until, to my horror, when the smell got too strong to ignore, I realized what the stench was: death.

Where was it coming from? I couldn't tell. Even through its increasing stench, I ran, continuing to look for someone, *anyone*. Any church with people that could join in sharing the gospel.

After several hours, the odor became too strong to carry on. It was unavoidable. Helplessly, I ran into one last church only to discover the source of this horrifying smell.

The pews of the church, once adorned in beauty and spiritual life, had fallen away. Slumped over each pew were the decaying bodies of the members of the church, the smell of death as potent as ever.

The Revenant

My eyes filled with tears as I wailed over these dead believers slumped over in the very place they once sat and were inspired by the Word of God. *Maybe it isn't too late,* I thought in my dream. *Maybe I can find the pastor to help resurrect the church.* But when I ran to the stage to find the pastor, I saw his lifeless body at the foot of the pulpit, clenching his Bible to his chest.

My heart started beating faster as I made my way to the children and youth rooms. *They are the future of the church,* I thought. *Maybe they could help bring life back.* When I made it to the youth rooms, I fell to my knees. Rooms full of lifeless children and students sprawled out on the floor. There was no one to lead them.

The smell didn't stop. The death didn't cease. Church after church, stage after stage, room after room the stench lingered like a dark storm cloud in the middle of summer. Through my frantic searching, I finally realized that the churches were empty, and I needed to give up. I went back to the city to do what I could for the kingdom on my own, only to find all the lost people in the city had died as well.

Suddenly, I jolted awake and wiped the cold sweat from my forehead, the stench of death still lingering in my nostrils. As those traumatic events from my dream played back in my head, I was left with one thought:

What good is vision without action?

Little did I know, not long after that dream, COVID-19 would spread across the US, and this vision turned nightmare would become reality.

Day 3: Covid (church On Vision Intensive Debacle)

It's Come to This

They say 2020 has been a year of firsts, and I couldn't agree more. But the slew of firsts that rocked the modern church leaves my head spinning:
- We were forced to wear a mask outside our homes.
- The federal government encouraged us to not celebrate Thanksgiving and Christmas with family and friends.
- We were asked not to shake hands or get close to others.
- After 245 years of religious freedom, the government prevented churches from meeting to worship God together.

And worst of all, the church listened to these decrees and halted one of the most important characteristics of our faith, fellowship. If the year before you would have told me all of these things would happen, I never would have believed you.

But somehow, it has actually come to this.

COVID-19 actually managed to stop churches from gathering and had them depend on live stream to inspire and stimulate the body of Christ to live out their faith. Life groups stopped meeting in homes for fear of infecting one another and spreading a virus that has a 99% survival rate. The monetary giving to expand the mission of the local church practically disappeared, forcing pastors to be laid off and churches to close their doors. No one could visit the sick and elderly because people were scared to allow guests into their home. Outreach events connecting the lost to the local church came to a halt, because state officials prohibited gatherings of ten or more people. All the while, the homeless population grew. The rate of addiction to alcohol and drugs climbed. The suicide rate was at an all-time high. And domestic violence calls reached such a high volume, the local police couldn't even respond to them all.

Our world, our church, it's come to this. But where there is breath, there is hope. And the Spirit of God? It simply can't be stopped.

Unstoppable Fire

Our country wasn't the first to experience absolute corruption and separation in history. In fact, in ancient Rome, there wasn't a political system more corrupt. Hostile groups of people formed, causing division and chaos throughout the empire. Political systems and rulers were unstable and unreliable. Nothing could be trusted.

It isn't a far jump to say that the political climate in America today has some striking similarities to political climate in ancient Rome. In America today, hostile groups of people are forming just like they were in ancient Rome. Some hold signs with the candidate's name that they believe will lead our country into much-needed change. Others hold signs of the opposing candidate and chant for change as well. There are groups of people protesting racial injustice, some peacefully and some violently, but both begging for change. Vicious bullies hunt for arguments online, forcing their opinions and ignoring those that are different. Then there are the ever-passionate vaxxers or anti-vaxxers, maskers or anti-maskers. America knows the familiar feel of separation and divisiveness all too well.

So then how did the early church handle it? What can we, as the modern church, glean from the ancient church in a time so separated and corrupt?

One word that comes to mind is *unstoppable*. It's a word that describes our God the Holy Spirit—He simply can't be stopped.

In the second chapter of Acts we see that the Holy Spirit comes down on the day of Pentecost with fire and wind, just

Day 3: Covid (church On Vision Intensive Debacle)

like it was prophesied. Immediately, people from every nation came together and began speaking about the greatness of God in their own language. And the most unbelievable part of all, people of every language could understand one another. Out of their amazement and confusion, some thought they had drunk too much wine! But that wasn't the case.

You see, after Jesus presented himself alive to the disciples in chapter 1, He was now giving them the gift of his foreign presence—the Holy Spirit. And He didn't just give His Spirit to the Jews or only to the men. No! The Bible says He gave the Spirit to people of every nation under heaven, male and female, rich and poor. The Spirit came down like an unstoppable fire. God poured out His Spirit on His people. In response, they spoke in a foreign tongue, had visions, repented, and were baptized. About three thousand people came to know Christ.

One thing I don't want you to miss is the group of people that were there at Pentecost. It was a very diverse group of people. We're talking about dozens of different cultures and tongues with different beliefs. Different backgrounds. Different stories. Different opinions about the world. And yet, here they were united under one tongue and one purpose. Not even their greatest differences could stop God's mighty spirit from bringing them together.

Why? Because the Spirit of God is unstoppable.

But it didn't end there. After they were saved, *they were together*. They learned about God together through the apostles' teaching. They broke bread together. They saw many spiritual signs and growth together. They gave together. They attended temple together and had dinner in each other's homes. They enjoyed each other's company. And through this community of believers, through this *togetherness*, many more came to know Christ. Despite their worldly differences, they were absolutely united in the only thing that mattered: Christ in them.

Why? Because the Spirit of God is unstoppable.

The fellowship that the ancient church had as a body was something that gave them richness of life. It allowed their church to thrive and brought many more to know the gospel. It's what helped spread the Word to the ends of the earth. This fellowship was like a rushing river to their parched spiritual ground.

During the pandemic and political turmoil in America, our fellowship as Christians was scarce. It was hard to remember the last time we were able to comfortably dine in other's homes, gather as one body, and simply live our Christian lives as one church. But the truth is that God did not intend for us to live that way. If we as believers want to revive the dead parts of our church and bring them back to life, we must come together.

We must sing songs of praise together as a church body. We must pray together in the Spirit and share our burdens with one another. We must open our homes to one another and lift each other up. Why? Because we cannot do this alone. We aren't called to live this Christian life alone. Just like the early church modeled for us, we must do this together. Because the Spirit of God is unstoppable.

Gold, Silver, and Things that Shine

Day 4

"If I find in myself desires which nothing in this world can satisfy, the only logical explanation is that I was made for another world."

C. S. Lewis

"And all the people saw him walking and praising God, and recognized him as the one who sat at the Beautiful Gate of the temple, asking for alms. And they were filled with wonder and amazement at what had happened to him."

Acts 3:9-10

I recently heard a story from well-known former pastor Francis Chan. In the interview, he was discussing why he left his megachurch that he planted almost thirty years ago. As he described the millions of dollars it took to keep the church running and the lack of meaningful connection within the walls of the church, he also detailed another memory.

The Revenant

Chan talked about a particular memory he had of seeing a convicted gang member attend his church and get baptized. After some time, he noticed that the former gang member had eventually stopped attending. When he asked about it, he learned that the man decided to go back to his life in the gang because he found more community there than at the church.

That story stings. Probably because it hits a little too close to home. It seems that more and more churches have made it the norm to spend tens of thousands of dollars on, well, things. Things that are bright and shiny and beautiful, things like silver, gold, new sound systems, lighting gear, special effects technology, new facilities, graphics, and entertainment.

But as money is being spent, people are being forgotten. Relationships are disintegrating. Families aren't being served. Communities aren't being helped.

It seems too often churches today are taking their eyes off the very thing that allowed them to open their doors in the first place: the Savior. Instead of fixing their gaze on Jesus, they are focusing on things like titles. They're stuck on denominational preferences. Or the number of people in attendance. Or the lure of thinking bigger is better.

In Acts 3 God reminds us that it was never about the distracting things like shiny silver or gold. It was always about the Savior.

The Lame Beggar

The third chapter of Acts is where Luke sets the scene. He tells the story at a temple by the Beautiful Gate. You can imagine why the gate got its name. At seventy-five feet tall, this temple gate was *beyond* beautiful. In fact, the ancient historian Josephus wrote, "It was the most beautiful gate in the world. More beautiful than

Day 4: Gold, Silver, And Things That Shine

all the gold and silver and anything inside it." Probably adorned with expensive gold and silver, this gate stood out among the rest. Many people would walk by this gate to admire its beauty and pray.

For that reason, there was a beggar lying outside the temple, searching for any money he could get. In that time, people would often use beggars to make money and prey on the generosity of bystanders. It is likely this beggar was being used to collect money in front of this massive gate, and when Peter and John walk by, they turned their gaze to the man.

As any beggar would, this man was expecting a monetary gift of some kind. Little did he know, he would receive a gift greater than money. Peter and John were about to set him free. Just not in the way he expected. "I have no silver and gold," Peter told the man, "but what I do have I give to you. In the name of Jesus Christ of Nazareth, rise up and walk!'" (Acts 3:6, ESV). I can only imagine the confusion the beggar had at that moment.

Are you serious?
I'm paralyzed, remember?
I just need some money!
How could you possibly gift me mobility?

But as it turns out, the beggar truly was healed. And it wasn't because of magic or trickery. It was only by the power of Jesus through Peter. But the beggar? When Peter told him to rise up and walk, he reacted much like the rest of us would at receiving such great a gift. He didn't believe it. His lack of faith glued his weak body to the ground. His unbelief locked him in place. Truly, this beggar was completely unaware of the goodness God could impart on him.

But Peter and John? Their faith was strong. They were sure that the power of Jesus could heal a lame man. How could that

~23~

beggar not see that? How could he not *believe* that? *Why won't he rise up and walk?*

You see, it wasn't enough for Peter and John to tell the man that they were Christians. It wasn't enough for them to proclaim the name of Jesus with their mouths and command him to walk in faith. No, that beggar needed something greater. He needed someone else—someone stronger—to carry his lack of faith. He needed someone to lean down, grab his hand, and pull him to his feet. And Christian, that is exactly what we are called to do.

On days when we see a person in need or struggling, the easy thing for us to do is tell them it's going to be okay. It almost rolls off the tongue: "God's got this" or "Keep the faith." And those things are true. But how different is it if we actually leaned down, grabbed a hand, and pulled a brother or sister to their feet?

Imagine how different the life of that convicted gang member could have been if this was the church he discovered, one that would truly see him, embrace him, and invest in him. This joining of life is exactly what Peter and John did when they lifted the beggar onto his feet. And once they did, he leaped and praised God with joy, just as anyone does when they have new faith.

Peter and John's eyes were not on silver or gold or the immaculate lure of the Beautiful Gate. Rather, their eyes were on Jesus, the author and perfecter of their faith. And because of that, they were able to witness the healing of a lame man and experience the joy that comes from someone believing in God through a transformational relationship with Christ. You see, our faith is perfected when we don't have our eyes on silver or gold but when we have it on the one who heals us.

Day 4: Gold, Silver, And Things That Shine

Sound Systems and Stained Glass

Years ago when I was a full time itinerant speaker, I was at an event in Gatlinburg, Tennessee. During the breakout sessions, I decided to take a walk through the downtown area. Passing all the tourist attractions—chairlifts, mini golf, and shops of sugary sweets, I stumbled upon a breathtaking church. The door was open, so I thought I would wander inside. This old church had wooden pews and paneled walls and vibrant stained glass windows glowing in the afternoon light.

Then, I spotted something near the altar. It was a piano. I love to play pianos in churches, so I sat down behind it and started playing. The notes echoed throughout the sanctuary, and about that time a lady approached me.

"That was beautiful!" she said, smiling brightly.

"Well thank you!" I responded as I stopped playing. "I saw the door was open, so I wandered inside. I have to say, I love these stained glass windows. They are incredible!"

"Aren't they?" she said, eyes gazing at the colorful glare from the windows. Her voice seemed to lose some excitement. "Believe it or not, those windows caused a lot of drama within our church."

"What do you mean?" I asked.

"Well," she explained, "Those windows split our church. Tons of people decided to leave all because of them. It's a real shame."

It is, I thought.

And while the story was surprising to hear, deep down, it really wasn't. Churches of all sizes throughout history experience unnecessary conflict. Why? Because without being careful, the people in the churches get focused on the wrong things. This dilemma spreads across all denominations and populations.

Since the beginning of time, people have been tempted to focus on silver and gold.

    Sound systems and stained glass windows.
    Entertainment and evangelism.
    Decoration and denomination.
    Loud music and liturgy.
    Money and missions.

It's a tale as old as time. But Acts 3, God reminds us through the words of Luke that the internal gift that Jesus gives is far greater than any external reward the world offers. This internal gift runs deeper than the number of people that responded to the altar call on Sunday or how much money you spend on stained glass or the dozens of catechism questions you memorize.

Perhaps the influential philosopher and priest Thomas Aquinas said it best. In 1260, he was visiting the Vatican where Pope Innocent II showed him all of the beauty and wealth inside the papal palace. While looking at all the riches, the Pope said, "'You see, the church is no longer in that age in which she said, *'Silver and gold have I none.'*'"

"True, Holy Father," replied Aquinas. "Neither can she any longer say to the lame, *'Rise up and walk.'*"

If we want to be a church that's truly after the heart and mission of Christ, we would do well not to focus on the silver and gold but on the power of the one who created it in the first place.

A Little Faith

While the phrase "silver and gold" reminds us of the ways money gets in the way of fully focusing on Christ, sometimes it represents the things that distract us from what matters. In Acts 16, Paul and Silas are beaten with rods and thrown into prison

Day 4: Gold, Silver, And Things That Shine

for casting a spirit out of a woman in the name of Jesus. While in jail they begin singing hymns and praises to the Lord. All of a sudden an earthquake shakes the jail and opens the gates of the cells. The guard draws his sword, ready to kill himself because the prisoners were going to escape. At that moment, Paul says, "'Do not harm yourself, for we are all here'" (Acts 16:28, ESV).

Their focus on Christ and honesty in the midst of an escape opportunity moved the guard to his knees. Paul and Silas actually won the heart of the very guard who was more than likely responsible for beating them before throwing them in chains. In turn, his entire household was saved. You see, Paul and Silas knew that that moment was a Jesus moment. They resisted focusing on the silver and gold and instead focused on the Holy Spirit.

The Holy Spirit has a life-giving power to prompt, heal, and move individuals. My hope has always been to raise our family in obeying the Spirit's call. That's why since we started having kids, my wife, Amy, and I have shared the desire to bring them into the mission field at a young age. Our oldest, Malachi, was first to get to experience a mission trip with Amy. They flew to the inner city of Johannesburg, South Africa to share the gospel. Once they arrived, the ministry team there took them to squatter camps, which are essentially makeshift neighborhoods. But not the kind that you're envisioning in the United States. No, these neighborhoods are where starving people from other parts of Africa come to stay alive.

I'll put it this way. In the US, you might have a house made of vinyl siding or brick. In South African squatter camps, you might have a house made of mud clay walls, a tin roof, and dirt floors. In America, our neighborhoods are scattered with mailboxes, cul-de-sacs, and newspapers on driveways. In squatter camps, these neighborhoods are scattered with thousands of people, human waste, and trash everywhere.

The Revenant

The ministry team that Amy and Malachi were with decided to split up and minister to people in dangerous parts of the area. While they walked through the camp together, they saw sin's fingerprint on every corner. Where poverty lives so also does gambling, prostitution, and addiction. Sadly, it's not unusual to see the Enemy feed off weaknesses of the vulnerable, especially in areas like this. As they walked through this dangerous area, Amy noticed a man who was gambling. She felt the Lord's Spirit prompt her to pray for the man, so she stopped and prayed. While she was witnessing to this man, Malachi noticed a crippled little girl, probably nine years old, coloring on the ground outside, and the Spirit touched Malachi's heart at that moment.

That's when Malachi felt prompted to lay hands on this child and pray for her. So, he walked over to the girl and began praying to God. He asked for her legs to be strengthened. For her feet to grow strong. For her body to be healed. After the prayer, Malachi and another witness gazed at the child and said, "Stand up and walk!"

And just like the beggar in front of the Beautiful Gate, the child would not get up on her own. The witness told Malachi, "Let's help her to her feet and walk with her." They leaned down. Grabbed her hands. Lifted her up. And she began walking on her own! Everyone's gaze turned toward the child and the place became silent. You could hear a pin drop.

"This girl has never walked in her entire life," the interpreter said, stunned.

The faith that God planted in my son's heart brought life and healing to this little girl. He wasn't able to give her silver or gold. No, my son didn't offer her anything except Jesus. In turn, his faith sparked a little revival in the heart of the child and the villagers of that area.

Day 4: Gold, Silver, And Things That Shine

Because of faith, this little girl is a follower of Christ who was touched by her Master in the form of complete healing. You see, it was never about what a missionary could do in Johannesburg, South Africa. Rather, it was about what God could do through a young man with a little faith.

Silver and gold? They're beautiful and shiny and valuable. But what's even more costly and precious is the love of Jesus and the power of the Holy Spirit, His ability to change our lives, and the internal gift He offers us.

That's greater than any temporal gift.

What Burns Within?

Day 5

"Get on fire for God and men will come and see you burn."
John Wesley

"Now when they saw the boldness of Peter and John, and perceived that they were uneducated, common men, they were astonished. And they recognized that they had been with Jesus."

Acts 4:13

When was the last time you stood next to a fire?

Perhaps on a cold winter day, you stood near the fire and warmed your numb hands, the heat radiating off your face as the embers crackled and sizzled. Maybe you stood near a campfire with friends and family, roasting marshmallows and trading stories. For some, the first memories you recall when it comes to fire are of a catastrophe when the flames devoured everything in sight.

Fire is powerful.

Day 5: What Burns Within?

It has the fierceness to overtake a city and the capacity to save a wounded soul. In fact, in *The Revenant,* Glass uses fire to help him survive the bear attack. After the attack, he tries to drink water only to find it trickling out of a wound in his throat. He decides to burn the skin on his neck to create scar tissue. As it heals, it stops the bleeding in the neck. You see, fire can transform ordinary things into something extraordinary.

In Acts 2, we learned that God sends the Holy Spirit down at Pentecost as tongues of fire, completely overtaking the disciples. Like fire does, it completely transforms these ordinary people. Once the fire comes down, the ordinary disciples begin speaking in other tongues through the power of the Holy Spirit. From there, the message of the gospel is spread to Jerusalem. Pretty extraordinary, right?

That's the thing about fire. It's powerful. It's transforming. It's *extraordinary.*

And as Christians, this fire isn't something that's made on the outside with a match and some logs. No, this fire burns from within.

It's that relational pull you feel when you're singing a song of worship.

It's that passionate tug on the heart you feel during a moment of conviction.

It's the source of every word, action, and choice you make.

My question for you as a believer is this: **What burns from within?**

Ordinary Without, Extraordinary Within

Sit in boat. Throw net. Wait for fish. Repeat.
Stand on bank. Throw net. Wait for fish. Repeat.

The Revenant

This is the arduous life of a fisherman. These men weren't glamorous or revered. They didn't exude coolness or even a pleasant scent. Ordinary fishermen like Peter were just that. Fishermen.

But not to Jesus.

You see, back then, it would be laughable that someone as significant as Jesus would reach out to a man like Peter. No one saw any promise to invest in an ordinary person like a fisherman. But Jesus decided to take Peter and John under his wing. These disciples begin to build a relationship with Jesus—listening, witnessing, and learning from Him.

Peter drops everything in his ordinary life to follow Jesus, and in turn, becomes a bold witness of the gospel. In Acts 4, we see Peter teaching and healing people through the power of the Holy Spirit. And while the fire above Peter's head at Pentecost was gone, it still burned deep within his heart, which was stoked through time by listening to Jesus' wisdom and training.

And the crowds? They were blown away. They had no idea how an uneducated fisherman was able to do these things. But history shows that the fire for Christ within was never about education. Take Paul, for example. Paul was educated by Gamaliel, one of the most famous teachers of the law at the time. The Holy Spirit was working through him in countless ways, and his work for the gospel was outstanding. But even Paul needed to burn from within. He needed to keep that fire aflame to continue to do the Lord's work.

In Galatians 1, Paul explained that he went away for three years to consult the Spirit of God and keep his fire burning. And he knew that even with all the education in the world, he couldn't keep that fire burning for Christ on his own. So he went away for three years to be in the counsel of the Holy Spirit.

Day 5: What Burns Within?

God doesn't need a perfect campsite to spark a fire. He doesn't need someone extra qualified, extra educated, or extra good. He simply needs your heart, burning with love for Him. And as you grow in spiritual maturity, that small ember from above has the power to spark a flame in your soul, ready to glorify the one who put it there in the first place.

Faith as Bold as Fire

There's nothing like the rejuvenating heat that fire gives to a cold body. Once powerless and shaking, flames can melt away all signs of insecurity.

But before this rejuvenating fire is set ablaze in Peter's heart, he is standing in a courtyard warming his hands by a fire. He stands shivering outside of the High Priest's house, where he denies being a follower of Jesus three times. There, his confidence falters like the waning flame of a dwindling campfire.

Then in Acts 4 we see a totally different version of Peter. He is standing in front of the same Sanhedrin council that convicted Jesus. Only this time, Peter's fire isn't warming his hands but consuming his heart! Peter stands boldly in front of the ruling class of aristocratic Jews, the Sadducees, after healing a lame man.

In many ways, the Sadducees were enemies of the early Christian church after Jesus died. They were deeply disturbed by what Peter did and said. After all, they controlled everything that went on in the temple, including priestly duties. They didn't believe in miracles, life after death, or the spirit world. But that did not deter Peter and John's boldness. Even after the Sadducees had Peter and John arrested, about five thousand people heard and witnessed what they were saying and came to faith. You see, the fire of the Holy Spirit *always* breeds boldness. It produces an all-consuming flame that can move you into prayer and action, impacting the world for the kingdom.

At a conference in Pigeon Forge, Tennessee, where I was speaking, a leader asked for prayer for his baby grandson who was less than a year old. At the time, H1N1 flu was going around, and the baby had contracted the virus. About a week after the conference, the leader called to tell me that his grandson was still suffering.

"Christian, I don't know what to do," he cried with a trembling voice. "My son-in-law is overseas in the military and can't get back to see his son. I am at a complete loss. Could you please keep praying?"

At that moment, I felt the Holy Spirit burning in my heart. I knew what I had to do.

"I need to go see him," I declared.

Before hitting the road on the four-hour journey, my boldness was quickly met by skepticism by many around me. And I'm not even referring to non-believers who heard I wanted to travel hundreds of miles to pray for a baby I'd never met. I'm talking about believers in my life.

But you just got home.
That's a long way to drive, Christian.
Can't you just pray from where you are?

For some reason, I decided to lean into the Spirit's prompting and make the trip to the hospital. When I got there, the sounds of the mother's weeping echoed off the sterile walls, along with beeps from the many machines. The baby was hooked up to more wires and tubes than I'd ever seen in my life. Upon arriving, I anointed him with oil, prayed for him vigorously, and read the Bible until it was time for me to go.

Day 5: What Burns Within?

On the way home, my phone rang. I immediately heard screaming and weeping from the other end of the line, and I knew it was the mother.

"Christian!" she screamed, "He's fully alert and receiving food!"

My mouth hung open in disbelief. This child was healed and on the road to recovery!

That compelling fire from God that was put in my heart that night was not for nothing. It was a prompt just for me, so God could do a small miracle in the life of a child. If I had relied on the spiritual flames of others to ignite my action, I would never have driven to the hospital. And while those people had good intentions, I'm not called to listen to people.

Well-intentioned people will tell you just to skip this Sunday. They might tell you not to give away that money. Or not to reach out to that person in need. But when it comes to our faith, we cannot allow people with different levels of intensity to blow out our flames. Instead, we must listen to the One who ignites them. And when He does, boldness like Peter is sure to follow.

Stoking the Fire Within

I once heard a pastor quote a statistic that absolutely blew me away: Almost eighty-seven percent of people who give their life to Christ do it before the age of eighteen.

After that, only thirteen percent of people come to Christ.

This *internal* and *eternal* training starts as a child, but from there, it goes in one direction or another. Your fire has the ability to grow stronger or burn out. That's why no matter if you are eighteen or eighty-one, you must focus on what burns within you.

So, I ask again. *What burns within you?*

The Revenant

A mother and father of three will push their kids to be involved and excel in school, sports, social events, and other extracurricular activities but will hardly press the issue when they wake up Sunday morning too tired to go to church. They can find their fire in Proverbs 22:6, "Train up a child in the way he should go; even when he is old, he will not depart from it."

An entrepreneur will spend on average sixty hours a week building his dream company to financially purchase all the things this temporary life has to offer but finds it hard to give to the local church that makes investments in the eternal. He can find his fire in the story of the rich young ruler in (Matthew 19:16-24). He is given an eternal invitation by Jesus but sadly walks away because he chose to keep chasing the temporary things of this life.

Much like an abandoned campfire, our hearts grow old and cold. Many of us accept Christ in burning anticipation, but as time goes on our fire gets weaker and weaker. And without maintenance that fire will eventually burn out. Or it will burn for something else.

If we want to live a life burning for Christ with hearts on fire for the things of eternity, we must stoke the fire within. Our fire is both sparked and stoked through prayer. Famous evangelist R. A. Torrey writes, "Pray for great things, expect great things, work for great things, but above all pray." Prayer is the foundation of our lives and the way we can recognize God's greatness—the way we keep our fire burning.

And while you can't go back in time to when you were younger or when your faith was bolder, you can start *right now* in growing a life of faithfulness, praying for the Spirit to burn in your heart. Only then can you live a life worthy of your calling, hearts set ablaze for the one who paid it all.

A Faith That Gives Life

Day 6

"The church is not a theological classroom. It is a conversion, confession, repentance, reconciliation, forgiveness, and sanctification center, where flawed people place their faith in Christ, gather to know him and love him better, and learn to love others as he designed."

Paul David Tripp

"Then Peter said, 'Ananias, how is it that Satan has so filled your heart that you have lied to the Holy Spirit and have kept for yourself some of the money you received for the land? . . . You have not lied just to human beings but to God."

Acts 5:3-4, NIV

"What's in a name?"

Clearly, Shakespeare missed the memo in his famous play *Romeo and Juliet*. Everybody knows that a name is anything but irrelevant. People use names to make the important things stand out in a world filled with endless words. Names help us identify and connect. When a baby is born and gets the family name, it says that this baby belongs. When the parents give the baby a name, it sets the tone for the rest of the child's life.

Think about it.

In the Bible, God changes Abram's name to Abraham, Sarai's name to Sarah, Jacob's to Israel, and Simon's to Peter. These names give them new hope. They're a prayer for what's to come.

My name is Christian.

Most people don't need any education on what that name means. Pretty obvious, right? Follower of Jesus Christ.

I guess you could say that my parents had some big hopes and prayers for me when I was born. After all, our Christian faith was the most important thing for my parents, my parents' parents, and my ancestors before that.

See, I grew up in Kannapolis, North Carolina, where around a hundred years ago my family donated land, lumber, and building materials to build the First Wesleyan Church. Today, my cousin and her husband pastor the church, and my aunt still plays the piano there every Sunday! My parents knew what was important, and they wanted me to grow up in an environment dedicated to Christ. They did everything they could to invest in my spiritual growth and my walk with the Lord.

Throughout my childhood and teen years, it seemed like I was really living up to my name. I sang in the children's choir and went to summer camp. I was baptized at the age of twelve. I was an acolyte and wore the white robe with the yellow sash, proudly carrying the candle into the sanctuary. I went to a Christian school and played baseball at a Christian college. I had a churchgoing pedigree stretching back for generations.

My name suited me.

It wasn't until 1987 that I realized that Shakespeare might have been onto something when on the side of the road at 4 a.m.

Day 6: A Faith That Gives Life

without fuel, keys, or an ounce of hope, I realized my name was irrelevant on its own. But I'm getting ahead of myself.

What's in a Name, Really?

In Acts 5, we meet Ananias and his wife, Sapphira, who were members of the early Christian church in Jerusalem.

This couple had meaningful names that preceded themselves. In Hebrew, Ananias means "gracious." In Arabic, Sapphira means "beautiful." Much like my own name, Ananias and Sapphira's names held potential for good things. But things started to go awry when this couple sold a piece of property. They both decided to give only some of the money to the apostles but say they were giving it all. Ananias marched down to the disciples and put some of the money at their feet, claiming that was all of the money. When Peter found out about this, he couldn't believe how they lied to God.

And as soon as Peter confronted Ananias about his dishonesty, he fell down dead on the spot. The shock of his sin being found out was just too much for Ananias. A few hours later, Sapphira arrived at the scene and was confronted by Peter about the land. After she lied about the price to conceal the money for herself like her husband did, she too fell dead.

God's wrath was so great that these people literally dropped dead for their deceit and selfishness. Peter didn't accuse Ananias and Sapphira of lying to the people of the church, but to God himself. The couple's faith in God's provision and goodness was completely absent! If Ananias and Sapphira had *real* faith, they would have given everything they had and would have been given life. Instead, they faked generosity and attempted to deceive the Lord, which ended in death. This is known as one of the most frightening stories in the Bible because it shows how even people with well-meaning names can fall—and fall hard.

When we rely on our prestigious names or backgrounds or denominations to justify our faith, it's easy to fall into sin. So often when I talk to churchgoers, they always seem to say first, "I'm Baptist" or "I'm Methodist" or what have you. There always seems to be a title to justify their faith on the outside. But our faith runs deeper than the names on the church sign.

See, Ananias and Sapphira were given names that pointed to great expectations that they did not live out. But what's true is their faith was never about their name or their background or how they appeared to be on the outside. True faith is inside out, not outside in.

Pontiac Firebird Kind of Faith

To be honest, the faith I had in my childhood and teenage years wasn't unlike the faith of Ananias and Sapphira. One that appeared bright and burning on the outside with all of my titles and works but was truly dull on the inside. I didn't know what it meant to live up to my own name.

As I became a young adult, my faith did what faith is bound to do when it's grown on the outside and not the inside—it burned out. Instead of chasing the things of God, I started chasing drugs, sex, and a life of pleasure. In 1987, some drugs I took started messing with my heart, and I had to spend a night in the hospital. When I got out of the hospital, my dad came and found me living homeless in Myrtle Beach, South Carolina, and got me a job in Charlotte, North Carolina, where he was the manager at a Honda dealership. One night they shut the dealership down and threw a big party for the employees with alcohol and drugs. Because of my addictions and recent experiences, I decided to leave the party

Day 6: A Faith That Gives Life

and head back home. I jumped on my motorcycle and headed back home. On the way I ran out of gas on Harris Boulevard (a.k.a. the worst and busiest part of Charlotte). After spending my last twenty bucks on a taxi and a gallon of gas, I hopped on my bike only to realize I had left my keys in the taxi.

That's when I lost it.

It's as though everything wrong I had ever done just fell right on my shoulders. Every mistake I ever made, every person I let down, every earthly pleasure I indulged—all of it—came crashing down. Like the rushing wind of a hurricane, my sin completely swept me to my feet, leaving me with nothing.

I'd been to jail. My friends weren't trustworthy. I had no education because I quit school. And now, there I was, on the side of the road with no money, no keys, no hope. It felt like rock bottom. For some reason I started praying. And for the first time in my life, I meant it. See, there's a difference between praying a religious prayer and praying a prayer from the heart. This prayer came from deep inside, and looking back, I now know it was where my faith was built.

I told God, "Look, I don't really believe in you. But I want to. I don't see you. But I want to see you. If you're really the God of love, help me know that I'm loved, and I will serve you with everything in my life."

This prayer didn't come from Bible class or my parents or my choir director. This prayer came from within. I wanted to learn what it meant to actually live up to my name.

When I opened my eyes after my prayer of faith, the very first thing I saw was a navy-blue Pontiac Firebird that had pulled over next to me. The driver rolled down his window, and I immediately saw a Bible on the passenger side seat.

My mouth hung open in disbelief.

The driver of the Pontiac Firebird was a black man who chose to pick up a random white kid on the side of the road at 4 a.m.

This man told me the Holy Spirit prompted him to pick me up and tell me God loved me and so he did. We didn't talk much in the car, but we didn't need to. God had told me everything I needed to know through my honest prayer for faith.

Through this faithful man in a navy-blue Pontiac Firebird, He reminded me that even though I didn't believe in Him, He believed in me.

Even though I couldn't see Him, He could see me.

Even though my faith didn't measure up to my name, He died on the cross to measure up for me.

That's the kind of faith that brings things from death to life—the kind that doesn't come from a church choir or stained glass windows or brick and mortar. Sometimes, all you need is a prayer from the heart (and a Pontiac Firebird).

Playing Church

When the church today thinks about Ananias and Sapphira's abrupt demise, many of us cringe at how quickly God killed people for the sin of pride, lying, and greed. Let's face it; we do things like that daily.

Think about it. How many times do we walk into church telling people with a smile how great we're doing when really everything is falling apart? How many times do we tell ourselves we're sacrificially giving when really we aren't giving even a tenth of the first fruits of our labor? How often do we raise our hands in worship on Sunday but raise our voices in anger on Monday? We sin, thinking we get away with it. Pastor Donald Gray Barnhouse in Philadelphia once said that if the Holy Spirit still operated like He did in the time of Ananias and Sapphira, we would need a morgue in the basement and a full-time mortician. He wouldn't even allow the choir to sing certain hymns because he knew they didn't truly mean the words in their hearts. If this is how God still operated, He would be striking us down left and right.

Just as I did growing up in the church, many of us "play church" to honor God. On the outside, we look like perfect Christians. We lean on our involvement and biblical knowledge to justify our faith, but on the inside do we even know who He is?

In Joshua 7, God destroys the Israelite Achan and his whole family for his secret sin, just like Ananias and Sapphira. The Israelites were to destroy the entire city of Jericho because of its sin, sparing only Rahab and her family because she helped hide the Israelite spies. They were commanded by God not to take any of Jericho's belongings because they were accursed or devoted to destruction. But Achan's faith was much too weak to trust God. On the outside, he pretended to follow orders. But when no one was looking, he took a robe and some silver and gold from Jericho.

Obviously, Achan's sin was found out—as are all our secret sins at one point or another. And the result? It's brutal. Read it for yourself:

> And Joshua and all Israel with him took Achan the son of Zerah, and the silver and the cloak and the bar of gold, and his sons and daughters and his oxen and donkeys and sheep and his tent and all that he had. And they brought them up to the Valley of Achor. Joshua said, 'Why have you brought this trouble on us? The Lord will bring trouble on you today.' Then all Israel stoned him, and after they had stoned the rest, they burned them. Over Achan they heaped up a large pile of rocks, which remains to this day. Then the LORD turned from his fierce anger. Therefore, to this day the name of that place is called the Valley of Achor (Joshua 7:24-26, NIV).

~43~

The Revenant

It's clear in history that God doesn't appreciate disingenuous faith. Faith that is only on the outside produces an empty religion, playing church. Worshiping God becomes something on our to-do list not something we commit to out of genuine faith.

Don't get me wrong. Corporate worship is an amazing celebration of faith. But we must remember that it isn't the meat of our faith, which produces victories. Faith is way more than what we do on Sunday mornings; our faith is the stuff that's alive on the inside and happens each and every day.

As I write this, I'm pastoring a small church in Bluffton, South Carolina. A member in our community had a son who was walking and got run over tragically while walking down a highway. The mother was absolutely distraught and asked the church for some help. As a result, our small church made enough food to feed all the people at the fundraiser for the family. *This* is the church. *This* is real faith. What's going on inside the church matters way more than what's on the outside.

Ananias and Sapphira lost their lives for playing church. Achan and his entire family were stoned for playing church too. While we probably won't be struck down with lightning for our outside faith, it is a dangerous thing to play church. It can prevent us from knowing the fullness and greatness of God, something that no one wants to miss out on.

As I think back to that moment on the side of the road at 4 a.m. when there was nothing holy about me except for my name, I can honestly say I don't believe Jesus used that moment to bring me back to the church my family helped build. He didn't use it to get me back to tithing ten percent or singing in the choir. He used that moment to bring me back to an authentic faith. One that began with a simple and honest prayer, changing me from the inside out.

He did it for me.

He can do it for you too.

Answer the Call Before the Fall

Day 7

"Fear can paralyze us and keep us from believing God and stepping out in faith. The devil loves a fearful Christian."
Billy Graham

"Therefore, brothers, pick out from among you seven men of good repute, full of the Spirit and of wisdom, whom we will appoint to this duty."

Acts 6:3

When was the last time you had a disagreement with someone?

Perhaps it was as common as clashing with a coworker on how to complete a task in the office. It could have been with your children on whether or not they could go out with friends. Maybe you had conflict with a friend about something he or she said that offended you. Maybe it was as trivial as disagreeing with a spouse on where to eat for dinner.

Regardless of how big or small these disagreements are, we can all agree we face these bumps in the road daily. Humans are full of problems. We each are born with our own unique personalities, cultures, languages, and backgrounds that directly impact how we interact and respond to others. And quite frankly these unique traits also directly impact our potential to *clash* with others.

Unlike routine disagreements, like over whether to eat a burger for dinner or spaghetti, disputes in the church can have a much greater impact. Conflict in the church pulls believers' focus away from the things that matter. In Acts 6, God does not gloss over these problems in the church. Why? Because our teams, neighborhoods, families, friends, health, and political systems are all *full* of problems. So the church will be too.

Even the first century church was full of problems, no matter how organized they might have been. When some disputes began to break out among believers, the twelve disciples, despite their imperfections, knew they needed to be ready to settle the issues. This passage of Acts reminds us that it's not a matter *if* church problems exist, but rather *how* we look to God's blueprint for the church in the midst of these problems.

Be Prepared

The disciples knew that when it comes to humans, sin is always in the midst: gossip, backbiting, affairs, addictions, lies; the list is long.

No one, no matter how holy he or she may appear to be, is exempt from the effects of the fall. That's why the twelve decided to assign seven people to help serve the needs of the widows, possibly for all seven days of the week. Acts 6:3 says, "Therefore, brothers, pick out from among you seven men of good repute, full

Day 7: Answer The Call Before The Fall

of the Spirit and of wisdom, whom we will appoint to this duty." They need not be only spiritually minded, but practically minded too. These leaders needed to be able to handle worldly disputes and conflicts in wise ways.

Thankfully, the disciples knew that the church desperately needed to be prepared for the call of God *before* the fall. They learned their lesson in the famous story of the fishes and the loaves when the disciples wanted to send a hungry woman away who needed to feed her child. Probably starving, this woman would have had nowhere else to go. But Jesus had compassion on the crowd. The disciples said to him, "Where are we to get enough bread in such a desolate place to feed so great a crowd?" (Matthew 15:33). And Jesus went on to feed thousands with just seven loaves and a few small fish. He couldn't send them away hungry. That day, the disciples learned not to send people away but to make a way for people. They answered God's call before they fell away.

Similarly, we as Christians must be prepared to be the hands and feet of Christ to our church and community. We need to be prepared to do so before allowing the Enemy to convince us otherwise. Dr. Nathaniel van Cleave says, "If you preach for one hour to 100 people and are not prepared to do so, you wasted 100 hours of God's time."

Our mission is every day, all day—not just for the few hours a week we spend at church or serving in youth groups. The Spirit is *always* at work within us. And the work we do to be prepared for the call is no small thing. So how do we prepare? Look to the example of Jesus.

Through the example of Jesus, the disciples learned it is crucial that we make wise decisions on the front end to ensure the church's healthiness. The disciples chose men they could trust to lead and settle any disputes. Therefore, we must be prepared to maintain our church's healthiness too. We need to know who we're serving with and make relationships with the people in our churches. With prayer, we'll be able to rely on the wisdom from the Holy Spirit to select wise people in leadership.

When we're prepared before times get tough or temptation overwhelms us, we'll be prepared to answer the call.

Be Mindful

Many of the revered people in the Bible were not brand-new Christians when they messed up. On the contrary, several of them had learned and heard from God himself. For example, David, a man after God's own heart, still committed adultery. Ananais and Sapphira still lied to God. Peter still practiced hypocrisy. Noah still got drunk. Samson still became prideful. Moses still got angry.

The point is, the problem within the church remains the same: *we are all sinners.*

The church is absolutely full of them, because it's full of people. If we aren't mindful and aware of our own sinfulness, it has the ability to divide us further apart from God.

A recent example of this in the modern church is former megachurch pastor Carl Lentz of Hillsong NYC. While pastoring a campus of this Australia-based megachurch in Manhattan, Lentz began experiencing pastoral burnout. He began having an affair with a woman who was unaware of who he was. When she found out he was a married pastor, she spoke out against him. Afterward, Lentz was fired and left the church, along with many congregants in his wake.

Not long after this incident, Brian Houston, the co-founder of Hillsong Church, resigned after he was accused of having inappropriate relationships with women. This type of sad reality leaves a bad taste in the mouths of thousands of people viewing the church. No one wants to see a person they look up to, admire, and listen to fall that hard. It's bound to leave scars on people's minds and hearts.

Without a doubt, there are flaws in churches all over the world. There are problems in megachurches and start-up churches. There are issues in cathedrals and arena-sized sanctuaries. And if we're waiting for great leaders to bring solutions to these intrinsic problems, the church itself will fall. But if *everyone* gets involved in the call of the Spirit before the difficulties arise, the church can sustain. She can be healthy and strong and radiant, just as Christ intended her to be. It's not about one person. It's about all of us joining together in this big call to believe and live out the gospel.

Be Productive

If the church is like a lion, the Enemy is like a hyena, prowling in the shrubbery just waiting for the right moment to pounce. His favorite pastime is drama, and his choice sport is fear. But above everything, the Enemy loves to divide.

The early church in the book of Acts was filled with two different types of believers: the Hebrews and the Hellenists. Acts 6 tells us about a complaint that arose against the Hellenists by the Hebrews. In ancient Jerusalem, the Hebrews were local and spoke Aramaic. Hebrew believers were seen as "holier than thou" by the Hellenists. Meanwhile, the Hellenists were Greek-speaking people from the diaspora (dispersed Jews living outside of Israel). Hellenist believers, due to their Greek culture, were seen as unspiritual.

In Acts 6, we see the Enemy trying to divide the church with a keen tactic called complaining. In this case, he tries to use unintentional harm to stir up drama among fellow believers. You

The Revenant

see, the early church deeply valued serving its widows because they were alone yet still expected to faithfully serve the church. In the eyes of the Hellenists, the Hebrew widows were being given better treatment than the Hellenist widows. While this might not have been intentional, it still caused much strife between the two groups. Satan loved the division. And such division happens in our modern churches too.

We are divided over how to worship. Over how to raise kids. Over what to preach about on Sundays. But the truth is we must step up to the call of God in our churches. We all have a part to play in fixing the issues in our church families.

You know what else is true? Both the Hebrews and the Hellenists were *Christians.* Both groups of people followed Jesus and looked to him as the Messiah! Still the Enemy divides. Even when it comes to Christians in the same church. He loves bickering, murmuring, and complaining among believers. It's no shock to me, and I'm sure with your own church experience, it's no shock to you.

To submit to the call of God within our church, however, we must answer the call before the division comes. That is, we must be productive with our words and actions and teaching. Our actions must speak louder than our words.

You don't have to be a famous pastor or church leader to rise to the call that God has set before you. In Acts 6, Stephen was chosen to serve the Lord in the church, and there is absolutely no indication that he was better or smarter than any of the other Jews. Stephen might have been a simple, average human who wanted to make a difference in the world around him. And God used him. Not for his abilities or lofty dreams, but because of his immense faith and sensitivity to the Spirit. You see, Stephen stepped up to the call.

Day 7: Answer The Call Before The Fall

And so can we. It is game on. *Now* is the time to rise and change the world around you for the better. Just as the Lord prepared many before us, He is preparing you. He has called *you* to be productive in the mission of the gospel. Your neighbor can't do it for you and neither can your own abilities. But through the Holy Spirit, you can answer the call.

It's time to buckle up. The ride isn't easy, but it will be well worth it.

Small Things Made Great

Day 8

"Many small people, doing small things, in small places, can change the world."

Eduardo Galeano

"But he, full of the Holy Spirit, gazed into heaven and saw the glory of God, and Jesus standing at the right hand of God."

Acts 7:55

On long and stressful weeks when my wife and I need a good laugh, we'll sit down together and watch a funny movie. Every now and then, we'll turn on the movie *Shazam*. Have you seen it?

It's about a boy named Billy who is abandoned by his family and becomes a nuisance to Child Protective Services. With the help of his handicapped best friend, he discovers that he has superpowers by saying the word *shazam!* Even though he becomes a real superhero, Shazam doesn't discover his greatness until he learns to use his powers for good.

Day 8: Small Things Made Great

It's another movie that teaches the classic theme that no matter how small or insignificant you may be, you're still capable of great things.

That is, with a little power.

When Billy says "shazam," he's struck with a bolt of lightning that gives him power. From then on, his world is forever changed. He's able to do things that aren't so small anymore. He's able to be someone that's not so insignificant.

See, power begets glory. It changes something small into something great.

While the Bible isn't filled with superheroes and magical bolts of lightning that make people powerful, it is filled with ordinary people that are made great through the power of the Holy Spirit. In Acts 6, we read about Stephen who was filled with the Holy Spirit. He was chosen to serve tables, a role that is often considered demeaning. But in Acts 7, small and insignificant Stephen does something that changes the course of history.

His story begins with the God of glory. And make no mistake, it will end with the glory of God.

A Crack in the Door

In the first several verses of Acts 7, we read the words Stephen preached to the Sanhedrin council after being accused of speaking blasphemous words against Moses and God. It was a moment when the Holy Spirit empowered him to speak clearly and boldly, proclaiming the truth in a way others could truly understand. That's when Stephen began essentially preaching Old Testament history as a way to remind the Sanhedrin council about what they seemed to have forgotten.

Stephen's door to share the gospel did not have to be fully open. He only needed a small crack to take this opportunity. And sure enough, he seized it to defend the message of God and the law of Moses. His words were big and powerful and true, pointing directly to the God who called him to stand up.

He boldly reminded the Sanhedrin of the promise of Abraham, and how the God of glory appeared to him, telling him he'd be the father of many nations even though he had no children. He pointed out how God was with Joseph even when his brothers sold him into slavery. Then, he talked about the life of Moses, and how he was rejected by Israel. Forty years later, God appeared to Moses in a burning bush and commanded him to deliver Israel. Stephen continued preaching until he finally called out the council for being "stiff-necked" or acting just like their forefathers acted.

I, too, had a small opening to share my testimony a couple weeks before Easter recently. I was approached by a young lady at a coffee shop where I always start my day. As we started talking, the story of Stephen came to mind.

"Hi, sorry to bother you," she said, "You're a pastor, right?"

"That's right," I replied.

"Do you do grief counseling?" she asked as her eyes wandered slowly down to her arms and then back up to me. The scars on her wrists and forearms told a story of pain, trauma, and darkness. My heart immediately ached for the depression this young lady was going through.

Here was my small moment. My crack in the door.

"Well, I can counsel, but I think we have multiple women at the church that would love to connect with you. For now, could I share my testimony?"

The tears ran down her face as I relayed my wild past, drug use, and that pivotal moment in my faith when I surrendered my life to Jesus. I told her how Christ changed my life, and that He

Day 8: Small Things Made Great

loves her. After we chatted for a few more minutes, I invited her to church on Easter Sunday. She agreed to come.

A few days later, I sent some reminder texts with our church's address and service times. Her replies slowly began to diminish as the days went on.

Surely, she will show up, I thought, *especially because God opened the door a crack for me to share my testimony.*

Easter Sunday came and went with no sign of her. I decided the least I could do was send her the link to the sermon on Sunday, and if she felt like watching it, she would have it. That's when I got this reply:

> I'm sorry, I don't think I can attend any services. I'm not Christian and there are a lot of beliefs I don't believe to be true. I will find my peace elsewhere.

Oh man!

That was not the text I was expecting. I shared my testimony, just as Stephen boldly shared the truth to the council. I seized the small opportunity to stand up for Christ. Why hadn't she come to church? Why didn't she watch the sermon? And if she did, why didn't she believe it to be true? Were my words not compelling enough? Did I misread the opportunity to share my testimony?

The truth is Stephen's boldness didn't turn out the way you'd expect either. Even though he stood up for the gospel and did what God asked, he was still killed.

In fact, the events are pretty ugly.

The Sanhedrin stood there, mouths hanging open, shocked by Stephen's audacity to condemn them in such a brave manner. The Bible says they were enraged, cut to the heart, and convicted by the Holy Spirit. They gnashed their teeth in anger. But before they charged at Stephen and stoned him to death, Stephen saw something.

He declared, "Behold, I see the heavens opened, and the Son of Man standing at the right hand of God" (Acts 7:56).

Whether it was a vision or heaven opening up for Stephen, the bottom line is that he saw Jesus standing at the right hand of God, not sitting but standing in solidarity with Stephen's actions and declarations. He had done what was right in God's eyes, even if it meant death. In fact, if Stephen had not stood up and laid down his life for Christ, most of the New Testament would not have been written. Why, you ask?

To quote Augustine, "If Stephen had not prayed, the church would not have had Paul." Every good thing for Christ that came out of Paul can be indebted to Stephen.

See, what started with the God of glory stirring in Stephen's heart ended with Stephen basking in the glory of God.

We can't control if the people who hear our testimonies receive it or not. That's not our role. Our only role is to be faithful to the call. To be sensitive to the prompts that the Lord puts on our hearts. To take the opportunity to share our faith, even if the door is barely cracked.

Stephen was willing to draw a line in the sand, even if it was the last thing he ever did. While sharing your story might not cause you to lose your life, it might, however, bring somebody from death to life.

Small People, Great Opposition

It's not typical that when someone hears the word *glory* that the term *opposition* comes to mind with it. Glory is the high honor one receives for their achievements. But for Stephen to come into the glory of God, he had to face brutal opposition in the form of rejection and death.

Day 8: Small Things Made Great

It seems as though all Christians must face some sort of opposition. Throughout history, we see how the cross divides people. It is very widely rejected among many people and often leaves a bad taste in people's mouths. Just look at Stephen. When God sent him to stand up to the council, he was stoned to death. But this kind of rejection of those whom God sends is not new. In fact, there is a pattern with the nation of Israel to reject the one God sends.

Joseph, son of Jacob and the patriarch that God selected, was rejected by his eleven brothers and sold into slavery. In Exodus, we learn about the Pharaoh who decided to drown all the Israelite children when they were born. But God chose to spare Moses. As he grew up, Moses was highly favored and very attractive. But after being given everything in the world's eyes, he chose not to be called the son of the Pharaoh's daughter, forfeiting all the earthly glory. He gave it all up for the glory of God. Stephen reminded the Sanhedrin that a person can have all the world has to offer and God still won't use them. But a person can lose everything in the world, and God can raise them up and give you the world.

Once Stephen finished his sermon to the council, they did what Israel had a history of doing. They rejected it. And again, they rejected the one God sent to deliver the message.

You see, opposition almost always comes to those whom God sends, no matter how big or small you are in the world's eyes. But the ones who are made great—the ones given the most glory in the end—they are the ones who continue to press on and honor God in the face of persecution.

Stephen's bold testimony was sealed in his own blood. He faced the ultimate persecution for the message he deeply believed in. For the God he deeply trusted. For the glory he knew was coming. And in the end, God honored him. He used Stephen's faithfulness to further the gospel in the world.

As I write these words to you, I often feel like I'm writing to myself. Because right now, it feels like I'm facing more opposition than glory in my own life. I know I'm doing what God called me to do in helping rebuild this old, traditional church in Bluffton, South Carolina. But in the midst of being here, doing the good work, I often feel defeated.

Instead of looking at my opposition as a negative, I choose to view it for what it is: the Enemy really, *really* wanting what I have. He is trying to rob me of every blessing God has for me, and I refuse to let him steal my joy. These attacks prove that God is doing something important in my life, and I will continue to make him the God of glory in it.

It's kind of like when a miner quits hammering away for valuable treasure. It means the mine is empty. When the Enemy quits hammering at our lives, maybe it's because our hearts are empty at that time. As Christians, we must remember to look at opposition and persecution as a treasure that God is tapping into. If you're like most and are facing some opposition for following God, remember that there is treasure in your heart that the Enemy wants to rob. Keep moving forward.

When the treasure is found, the glory of God will come with it.

Greatness in the Form of Chairs

I'm not sure anyone understood the concept of greatness coming in the small and ordinary more than my friend Stephan.

I met Stephan in Charleston, South Carolina, when I was a youth pastor in a church in the city. He was born and raised in Germany and was intellectually gifted. Stephan was sent to

Day 8: Small Things Made Great

be an engineer at a German-owned plant in Charleston at the age of nineteen. While Stephan wasn't small in stature (he was six feet eight inches), he was just another person like you and me who struggled with sin and wanted to grow in his faith. He wanted to get involved in the church and serve wherever he was needed.

"Well," I told him, "our youth group has about four hundred teens. You can help me set up chairs for our Wednesday night youth service."

I showed him how to line up the chairs and left him to it while I took a call on my phone. Somehow, time got away from me, and a few hours had passed. I jetted to the youth facility through a shortcut through the backstage area, thinking surely that Stephan had left hours ago. But before I busted in the room, I decided to peek through the curtain backstage.

There was Stephan, ruler in hand, measuring four inches in between each chair, praying over each one. This ordinary guy, this ordinary sinner, was on his hands and knees lining up the chairs, devoted to his role with such a high level of excellence. It brought me to tears. Stephan was worshiping the God of glory through his ordinary actions. He humbly accepted his role in the church with excellence. I ended up taking Stephan under my wing, and eventually he became one of my best leaders. When I moved to Charlotte, Stephen came to help get the church started but would later go back to his hometown in Germany to plant and lead his own church!

Mother Teresa said, "There are many people who can do big things, but there are very few people who will do the small things." Stephan was a person who did both. And by doing so, he was able to bask in the glory of God.

When your life is surrendered to the God of glory just like Stephen and Paul's and Stephan's lives were, you will surely

~ 59 ~

The Revenant

experience the glory of God. No matter how small and ordinary you may be. Because through small people, God can do great things.

Not For Nothing

Day 9

"What's done in the name of the Lord is not in vain. It's being remembered, recorded, and will be rewarded. Count on it."
Chuck Swindoll

"And there arose on that day a great persecution against the church in Jerusalem, and they were all scattered throughout the regions of Judea and Samaria, except the apostles."

Acts 8:1

Well, that was all for nothing.

If I had to bet, I'm guessing that's what most people thought when Jesus was crucified. He rode into Jerusalem on a donkey, palms waving and crowd cheering for this Savior who would somehow make a way for them.

And then He died.

Seemingly, it was all for nothing, but the plan was only at the beginning phase. After three days, Jesus would rise again, making an even more monumental moment in history than anyone could ever imagine. The resurrection would become the basis of our faith.

Was Jesus' death all for nothing? Quite the contrary.

When it comes to Stephen's death, I would also assume that the people likely believed his ministry was all for nothing. And at first glance, it's easy to see why. His ministry time was cut short and not many people were saved right away. Not to mention that the events following Stephen's death developed into more persecution of Christians.

But as time would tell, Stephen's death would be just the beginning of the persecution. Soon, many more Christians professing the gospel would be punished, banished, attacked, blasphemed, arrested, beaten, scattered, stoned, beheaded, and killed. "Saul was ravaging the church, and entering house after house, he dragged off men and women and committed them to prison" (Acts 8:3). Saul was relentless in his attack against Christians.

Two thousand years later kingdom work still means struggle. If we're honest, being active members of the modern church often feels like we're going against the grain. Satan will tempt us. With issues, whether they be with financial struggles, prodigal children, marital issues, gossip within the church, or even rejection from friends.

It is crucial to remember that amidst the inevitable struggle that comes with preaching the gospel, we must rely on the Holy Spirit.

Struggling for Christ is never for nothing. The apostles in the early church understood this, and it's why amidst the significant persecution, the gospel still spread. Today, in the age of the modern church, how can we continue spreading this gospel when wars are breaking out, people are being killed, friendships are being broken, and it just seems easier to quit?

Day 9: Not For Nothing

We can take it from those who went before us.

Deep Roots

As the persecution of the church came in all its fierceness and destruction after Stephen was stoned, it scattered everyone throughout Judea and Samaria, but not the apostles. Why? Because it's easy to scatter those with weak faith.

Think about it this way. When a storm comes through in all its fierceness and destruction, it leaves homes overturned and trees uprooted. The trees that are demolished are typically the ones that have wide roots, not deep ones.

But the trees with deep roots do not waver amidst the storm, and those with deep faith do not waver amidst persecution. They hold strong. Like the trees with deep roots, the apostles' faith was deep and wide and able to withstand more opposition through the strong power of the Holy Spirit. While most people were scattered, the gospel still was preached and spread amidst the heavy persecution.

To understand how to handle persecution in the modern church, we can look to the apostles in Acts 8. This chapter mentions the apostle Philip who was not scattered due to his strong faith. He decided to let the Spirit guide him in his ministry. (By the way, this is the same Philip who was chosen in Acts 6 to be a janitor.) In his calling, the Spirit led him to harvest the seeds that Jesus sewed before He died. And before I tell you where Philip went to preach the good news, let me give you a little backstory.

In the tenth century BC, there was a split between the monarchies of Saul, David, Solomon, and Rehoboam. Of the twelve tribes, ten tribes went north, and their capital became Samaria. The other two tribes went south, and their capital became Jerusalem. I like to think of these two separate groups of people as the original Hatfields and McCoys!

Anyway, time passed, and the Assyrians captured the ten tribes in the north. Then, they interbred the Jews with the other tribes that were captured. This group of people eventually became the Samaritans, which the Jews saw as half-breeds. They despised the Samaritans for this reason.

Well, in 303 BC, the hated half-blood Samaritans asked Nehemiah to allow them to help in rebuilding the temple. Because of their bloodline, Nehemiah rejected them. That's when they built their own temple on Mount Gerizim, the holy place where Abraham almost sacrificed Isaac. This spot is the very place Jesus went to stop all this separation and division among the peoples.

And Philip? When he was called to be a janitor, he accepted that role with obedience and grace, confident that the Lord would work through him somehow. And from being a janitor, he turned into a powerful preacher of God's word. He decided to pick up where Jesus left off in the same city Jesus visited.

See, Philip chose to preach to the very people whom everyone else rejected. He let his roots grow deeply into Christ. And through the Holy Spirit, he found value in what the world deemed as invaluable.

And then there's us in the present day.

Some of us are entrepreneurs. We will spend sixty hours a week building our dream companies to purchase all the things this temporary life has to offer. And yet we find it hard to give to our local church that makes investments in the eternal.

Some of us are young adults. We set our iPhones to wake us in the wee hours of the morning to climb rope, slam medicine balls, leap boxes, and pump iron in a forty-five-minute CrossFit workout that would tire the strongest of Roman Gladiators. But

Day 9: Not For Nothing

when it comes to making a morning worship service, we always seem to forget to set our alarms.

Some of us are midlifers. We binge watch an entire season of Yellowstone with Kevin Costner but will complain when the pastor goes five minutes over his thirty-minute sermon.

Some of us are parents. We push our kids to excel in school, sports, social events, and other extracurricular activities but will hardly press the issue when it comes time to go to a youth event at your local community church.

If *we* lived during the time of the early church, most of us likely would have scattered like those with weak faith. Our shallow roots would be uprooted in the storm in a heartbeat. But Scripture reminds us time and time again that in order to have faith like Philip, in order to spread the gospel, we must grow our roots *deep* into Christ. "Let your roots grow down into him, and let your lives be built on him. Then your faith will grow strong in the truth you were taught, and you will overflow with thankfulness" (Colossians 2:7, NLT).

When our roots grow deep into the faith we have as a church family, the kingdom can be lived out on earth as it is in heaven. The good news will spread. Like Stephen, our work will not be for nothing.

Hit Your Knees

I always say that when you do Acts 1:8, Acts 8:1 will happen.

Basically, if you receive power from the Holy Spirit to spread the gospel (Acts 1:8), then persecution is going to come (Acts 8:1). It's inevitable.

Take it from me.

As I pastored this church in South Carolina, I watched my mentor's wife die of mouth, jaw, and throat cancer. He took care

The Revenant

of her at night and cleaned out her trachea, so she wouldn't choke and die.

The condo I was living in was about to be sold, and I had no idea where I was going to live.

One day I got so stressed out about everything that I jumped in my Jeep to get away from it all. Of course, that's when my Jeep overheated.

My mother was suffering from Alzheimer's and often forgot who I was. In fact, the other day she called me and said, "I think you're a good looking man, and you'd make a great husband for the lady that takes care of me." The lady that took care of her is my wife. We've been together for over thirty years.

To top it all off, I sat at a restaurant by myself the other day, weeping into my hands. It felt like everything was going wrong, and I wondered if my ministering was for nothing. That's when I felt a friendly hand on my back and heard the kind server say, "It's going to be okay, Pastor Christian."

Sometimes, the struggle really does convince us our good work is meaningless. Philip most likely felt the same way, but it didn't stop him. He knew persecution was inevitable, as it comes with the territory of spreading the gospel. The truth is that if you're going to live this life and do ministry work like Philip, it's going to take complete compliance to the Holy Spirit. That's the only way anything worthwhile can come from our ministries.

In Acts 8, we're reminded that the Spirit—the one we rely on every day to press on—can't be bought. We read about Simon, a magician in Samaria who comes to be saved through the evangelism of the apostles Peter and John. Like many Samaritans, he is amazed with the miracles and also with this thing called the Holy Spirit. So amazed, in fact, that when he sees the apostles lay hands on people and the Spirit falling, he wants to buy that power.

Day 9: Not For Nothing

I can just imagine Simon's eyes turning into dollar signs like a cartoon character when he saw the miracles the Spirit was doing. Because Simon was focused on the wrong thing, he desperately desired the ability to lay hands on people. But as we know, the work of the Holy Spirit is not just another trick in a magic show. It's not a status symbol. And it certainly isn't something that can be purchased with money. Peter and John were quick to teach Simon that that's simply not how the Holy Spirit works. Check out Peter's response to Simon's foolishness:

> But Peter said to him, "May your silver perish with you, because you thought you could obtain the gift of God with money! You have neither part nor lot in this matter, for your heart is not right before God. Repent, therefore, of this wickedness of yours, and pray to the Lord that, if possible, the intent of your heart may be forgiven you. For I see that you are in the gall of bitterness and in the bond of iniquity." (Acts 8: 20-23)

Clearly, Simon was focused on the wrong part of greatness. He wanted to use earthly means to gain popularity and power but was quickly condemned. The corruption Simon showed is a caution for us to keep focused on the right things.

The Enemy is constantly throwing temptations at us to veer us off God's path. If we're not careful, we, too, will desire the wrong things like Simon did. How often are we more concerned with the appearance than the actual message being preached? How many of us show up to church on a Sunday as another box to check but are disconnected the entire service? How many times do we raise our hands in worship and forget what we sang the second our car leaves the parking lot?

The Holy Spirit is more than the trivial distractions that pry us away from sharing the gospel. That's why when we pray to the Holy Spirit, we must pray that He aligns our desires, words, and deeds with His own. Only then can we press on through our struggle in confidence that we aren't seeking the wrong things like Simon did

Rest assured, however, that in our struggle, we're not alone. God always finds a way to remind us of his faithfulness. Toward the end of Acts 8, the Spirit led Philip to a desert in Jerusalem. There, he met an Ethiopian eunuch riding in a chariot reading from the book of Isaiah. The book that includes the prophecy of Jesus. The one book, specifically chapter 53, the Jewish people can't do anything with because it discusses the crucifixion of Christ.

In the 1940s, the Great Isaiah Scroll was found on the northwest coast of the Dead Sea. This is the oldest copy of the Old Testament Scripture! All of the other books were damaged or fragmented *except* Isaiah—the book that prophesies the crucifixion! While some people have argued that Scripture is "too old" or "not translated correctly," these scrolls prove how accurate they truly are. They are hardcore evidence that we can find truth and stability in what God wrote.

The fact that God led Philip to this eunuch to bring meaning to the words was no accident. It was the plan all along. Later, this man was baptized and saved.

As I reflected with my own church on this chapter of Acts one Wednesday evening, I decided to try to model Philip's deep roots into Jesus. To take the experiences of an apostle to heart. The next morning, the first thing I did when I rolled out of bed was hit my knees. I vowed to keep going on in my ministry, even when it's sad all around me. As I prayed, I began to feel good about the fact that there is a struggle to what I'm doing, because it makes it that much more valuable.

Kingdom work is never easy. It's never seamless. It's certainly never carefree. But I choose to press on. I choose to hit my knees and let the Holy Spirit guide me like he did the apostles before me. Because that work I'm doing, the work you're doing, and the work our churches are doing across the world will not be for nothing. With the power of the Holy Spirit, it will result in joy.

In the Blink of an Eye

Day 10

"God changes caterpillars into butterflies, sand into pearls, and coal into diamonds using time and pressure. He's working on you, too."

Rick Warren

"And immediately something like scales fell from his eyes, and he regained his sight. Then he rose and was baptized."

Acts 9:18

There's something to be said about seeing things the way they really are. When you're a child and see a monster in a dark room, your mother turns on the light, and you see it was only a hat on a stand. When you're a teenager and your first love betrays you, you finally see their faults that were there the whole time.

Sometimes it takes a single moment to change the way we see things forever. Albert Henry Ross (1881-1950), a journalist and novelist who grew up in Stratford-on-Avon, England, and wrote under the literary pseudonym Frank Morison, had a

Day 10: In The Blink Of An Eye

moment like this while doing research for a book he was writing to disprove Christianity. Along the way, Ross claims he saw things differently than he had before. He confessed "one day that not only could he no longer write the book as he had once conceived it, but that he would not if he could."[1] In the midst of his research, God met Morison right where he was—smack in the middle of his doubt. In the blink of an eye, He was found. He ended up writing the book *Who Moved the Stone?* which is a defense of Christianity.

Evangelical Christian apologist and evangelist Josh McDowell has a similar story. He is an intellectual who struggled with the reliability of Christianity. That is, until he began doing extensive research following a challenge from a friend. He stated, "I spent months in research. I even dropped out of school for a time to study in the historically rich libraries of Europe. And I found evidence—evidence in abundance; evidence I could hardly believe with my own eyes."[2] Like Morison, God met Josh right where he was—smack in the middle of his doubt. McDowell put his faith in Jesus when he saw Him for who He really is.

According to Josh, if he was to disprove Christianity, the two biggest problems happened to be these:

> The resurrection. No other religious leader or god had *ever* been raised from the dead.

> The conversion of Saul. How could the greatest *opponent* of the church become the greatest *proponent* of the church?

---

1   Frank Morison, "Preface," in Who Moved the Stone?, (Gospel Truth Ministries, 1930), doi/url.
2   McDowell, Josh, "My Story: How My Life Changed," Cru.org, Cru, Accessed July 17, 2022, https://www.cru.org/us/en/how-to-know-god/my-story-a-life-changed/my-story-josh-mcdowell.html

~ 71 ~

Acts 9 focuses on this shocking conversion of Saul on the road to Damascus. This is known to be one of the most significant events in the Bible because it shows such an extreme change in character. *That* is the power of the gospel. The Holy Spirit has the power to change our hearts in the blink of an eye. And that is exactly what God wants to remind us of today.

CHECKMATE

If you've ever played chess, you know that a player cannot move their king out of being captured, they are in checkmate. There's no escape for the king, and the opponent wins the game.

C. S. Lewis compared Saul's conversion in Acts 9 to a game of chess. God was playing chess with Saul and maneuvering pieces of his life until he backed him in a corner and said, "Checkmate."

Here's the story.

Something amazing happened to Saul. A light from heaven shone on him, and he immediately fell to the ground. That's when the Lord audibly spoke to Saul, which was quite unusual. Of course, Saul was terrified at the voice from heaven and fell to the ground. Even though it was midday, when the sun shines the brightest, a brilliant light blinded Saul. He said it was brighter than the sun!

The Lord said, " 'Saul, Saul, why are you persecuting me?' And [Saul] said, 'Who are you, Lord?' And the Lord said, 'I am Jesus, whom you are persecuting. But rise and enter the city, and you will be told what you are to do' " (Acts 9:4-6).

In the American Standard Version, the Lord says, "Why are you kicking against the goads?" A goad is a long, sharp stick that pokes the back of an ox while plowing to make it go in the direction you want. It's designed to make the ox submissive if it starts going in the wrong direction. In this parable, Saul is the

Day 10: In The Blink Of An Eye

ox—stupid, stubborn, and going in the wrong direction. Jesus is the farmer—the wise leader who knows the way.

Just as Saul was blinded by his hatred against Christians, he was physically blinded by this bright light. But God loved him too much to let him keep going the wrong way and had to back him into a corner. In response to this terrifying encounter with the Lord, Saul responded with two very personal questions, one that shows a fully surrendered heart. He asked,

Who are you, Lord?

What would you have me do?

Pastor Rick Warren says that a purpose-driven life is knowing Jesus and what He wants you to do in life. That is where real life begins, which is exactly what Saul found in his conversion on the road to Damascus.

It is through the bright light from heaven that God reveals to Saul that light has more power than the darkness. After a life of violence and hatred toward those who believed in Jesus, Saul realized that this Jesus really *did* rise from the dead. He's alive now and He's alive with His people. Through the times in our lives that are full of despair, Jesus is right there with us, just as He was with Saul.

You see, God's loving pursuit of Saul reminds us that our conversion and salvation are not something we do on our own. Our salvation solely depends on God. It's something that God does in us, not what we do in ourselves. Anything we do is only a response to what God does through us.

This concept that was shown on the road to Damascus is one thing that separates us from any other religion. Josh McDowell said, "Christianity is not a religion. Religion is humans trying to work their way to God through good works. Christianity is God coming to men and women through Jesus Christ."[3]

---

3   McDowell, Josh, "My Story: How My Life Changed," Cru.org, Cru, Accessed

The Revenant

Just the other day, I got to church early and saw a woman outside of the church praying over one of our members. I stopped by and said hello, but I received no response back from her or her daughter. No one knew her, and something didn't sit right with me. Later, as I was preaching during the service I couldn't help but notice how she was responding to the message. She was making faces and gasping as she turned around to look at other people in the service. Quite frankly, it was very distracting.

After the service, she approached me.

"I don't know who called you to pastor," she huffed, "but you are *not* called to preach." She then went on to make judgmental statements about how the women in the church were dressed ungodly and about a man she saw smoking a cigarette outside before church. After a long conversation on all of the legalistic beliefs she held and the threat of hell that beckons those of our congregation, I finally had to be frank with her.

"You do not need to come back here for worship service," I stated. "We will only hold you back. This church is full of people like Saul who are in desperate need of God's love and grace. We are beautifully broken people only made right through the life, death, and resurrection of Jesus Christ not by a list of do's and don'ts."

When God revealed himself, Saul's eyes were opened to his wretched sin. And at that moment, Saul believed he was the worst person, the chief of sinners. He knew there was no one alive that could top his level of sin. But the best part is, that's who God goes after. Jesus isn't God of the perfect. He's God of the sinners. The God of you and me.

His love is so deep and so rich that His pursuit of us won't stop until He finally says, "Checkmate."

July 17, 2022, https://www.cru.org/us/en/how-to-know-god/my-story-a-life-changed/my-story-josh-mcdowell.html.

Day 10: In The Blink Of An Eye

The Power Of One

The apostle Paul wrote: "God causes everything to work together for the good of those who love God" (Romans 8:28). He works out the small pieces and the large ones. He ties up each loose end to make sure His will is done.

And in Saul's case, God handles every detail leading up to his conversion, even the message to Ananias. See, God told Saul to go into the city and he will hear what he must do (Acts 9:6). I'm sure there were dozens of questions buzzing around Saul's head, including, *Where will I hear my directions, Lord?* (And I'm sure he was hoping they didn't come in the form of another terrifying bright light!)

All the while, God was working out the details. Ananias was an ordinary man. God came to him calmly in a vision. He responded, "Here I am, Lord." God then instructed him to go to Straight Street and pray for no other than *Saul*, the guy who was killing all the Christians. When God reassured him that he would be telling Saul how much he would suffer on the Lord's behalf, I'm sure he felt more confident to do that. After all, he was justified for the things he did. The Lord told Ananias that Saul would be expecting him there, and Ananias didn't question his Lord's instruction. He willingly obeyed, trusting that God knew what He was doing.

And Ananias? He was only *one* person. But he made a huge difference in history. As a matter of fact, he was pretty much the hero in this story. Because of his faithfulness to God, Saul was immediately filled with the Holy Spirit and baptized. The scales were removed from his eyes, and he finally saw the Lord for who He really was—Jesus, the incarnate Son of God, the Savior of the world.

Later, when Saul preached to the Gentiles he went by Paul. In Paul's first letter to Timothy, he recalls his time as a sinner. He makes this powerful statement to Timothy: "Although I was formerly a blasphemer, a persecutor, and an insolent man; but I obtained mercy because I did it ignorantly in unbelief . . . However, for this reason, I obtained mercy, that in me first Jesus Christ might show all longsuffering, as a pattern to those who will believe in Him for everlasting life" (1 Timothy 1: 13, 16, NKJV).

Paul's conversion experience can be looked at as a *pattern* for believers, a pattern for us. Because of God's great mercy and the constant pursuit of us, we can share in Saul's experience. First, Jesus will pursue us in the middle of our sin, removing all barriers to get to us. It is then our choice to accept Christ as our Savior and wait for Him to do work in and through us. And with our salvation stories being modeled after Christ's work in Saul, we can also share in his testimony. Saul wrote to the Philippians: "I want to know Christ—yes, to know the power of his resurrection and participation in his sufferings, becoming like him in his death" (Philippians 3:10, NIV).

You can be found, even when you aren't looking. You can be saved, even if you appear unsavable. Jesus has the power to reach *anyone* and *everyone.*

He is the only One our soul needs.

Wall Destroyers

Day 11

"Sometimes you put walls up not to keep people out, but to see who cares enough to break them down."
Socrates

"So Peter opened his mouth and said: 'Truly I understand that God shows no partiality, but in every nation anyone who fears him and does what is right is acceptable to him.' "

Acts 10:34-35

Several years ago archaeologists found an ancient wall that is still standing in Caesarea. This wall was an underwater project launched by Pontius Pilot. It was meant to protect the other foundations from high tide near the city's edge. Somehow that long ago people found a way to pour mortar underwater to keep waves from pounding the city.

When you think about Rome, Nero, and everything they were building at that time, it's important to consider the spiritual walls that were being built as well. Just as the wall in Caesarea is still standing to this day, there are spiritual walls that the Enemy builds to this day. Perhaps one of the biggest walls the Enemy was building in Peter's heart at that time was between Jews and Gentiles by convincing Peter that the gospel was only for the Jews. See, typical Romans worshiped Roman gods, but there was a category of Gentiles who were God-fearers. These God-fearing Gentiles believed in the God of Israel but did not practice Jewish customs. To the Jews, these people were still not godly enough to live with them, befriend them, or even share food with them.

Jews had built a wall between themselves and the Gentiles. And today Christians do the exact same thing. We tend to separate ourselves from people as though our own holiness sets us apart.

I can't befriend those people. They're living a life of sin.

I can't understand those people. They're a part of a different denomination.

I can't love those people. They refuse to go to church at all.

But perhaps God has a bigger story to tell us, just like he did with Peter.

An Unlikely Faith

Years ago, a good friend of mine, Ephram Smith, told me about an itinerant speaking event he had in Minnesota. Before speaking, the pastor took him around the city to some of the worst places with the biggest need. The corners were filled with drugs, prostitution, homelessness, and filth. Many people had been gunned down and killed in these areas.

After the dark tour, the pastor asked Ephram, "So, what do you think about all this?"

He replied, "The biggest tragedy is that at every corner we came across, there was a church."

Day 11: Wall Destroyers

We like to put walls up between the holy and the hurting. It helps us keep up a clean image and makes us more comfortable. Peter was of the same mindset. After all, he was called Peter son of Jonah. In Greek, "son of" means "characteristic of." Jonah didn't want to go to Ninevah because he held a little racism in his heart. Maybe Peter was like Jonah because he didn't want to go to Cornelius for similar reasons. See, Cornelius was a centurion of the Roman army, a God-fearing Gentile whom most Jews would hate. Not in a million years did he think that Cornelius could come to Christ.

But God had different plans.

At the time, there were sixty centurions per legion. Cornelius was a fantastic leader, a risk taker, and the backbone of the legion. But what's more, he had great faith in Jesus and wasn't even saved. This man loved God but was excluded from the temple because of who he was. In a dream, God appeared to Cornelius and praised him for his generosity and strong faith. He told him to go to a guy named Peter and that he would tell Cornelius what to do.

Meanwhile, Peter was thirty-five miles away, and God spoke to him in a vision on a roof in Caesarea. In this vision, lots of four-footed animals and other odd creatures fly around him, and God commands Peter to rise and eat them. Peter's response?

"Not so, Lord."

Let's think about that for a minute. This disciple of God who was saved and following the laws of God told the Lord no because he believed the animals were unclean. And yet Cornelius, an unsaved Roman officer who was hated by most Jews of that time, when an angel of God calls his name, he says, "What is it, Lord?"

Two polar opposite responses by two polar opposite God-loving men.

Even though the enemy had created walls to separate these unlikely people, God still used them. Cornelius finds Peter, where he delivers the good news of the gospel to this centurion. Cornelius is filled with the Holy Spirit and baptized right then and there.

Sometimes, God works in unlikely people in the most unlikely of ways.

You First

In my temporary home in Savannah, I recently started renting the basement of a 1920s house in the heart of downtown. Above my basement area are two young college students attending Savannah College of Art and Design. I've met them a few times briefly and told them I was a pastor helping rebuild a church in the area. One day, I came home to a friendly note on the basement door. It said, "Pastor Christian, we wanted you to know we are a 4/20 friendly household."

I had to call them because I had no idea what that meant. Come to find out, it means they indulge in marijuana. I laughed as they told me and said, "Well, when I first met you, I already smelt it. It's all good; live your life. It's no problem for me."

A few weeks later, we all decided to go out to eat together at a vegan restaurant in Savannah. As we talked, one of the young women made it clear she was an atheist and that she was also a lesbian. My response?

"Cool! The lasagna looks so good here."

She seemed surprised, and we had a lovely conversation for the duration of the dinner. I got the opportunity to share my testimony and why I believe in the gospel, and she ended up deciding to come to church in a couple of weeks.

"I have to tell you, Pastor Christian," she shared with me a few days after the dinner, "All of our friends know you as the cool pastor."

I laughed and replied, "Well not to brag, but I *am* the coolest pastor."

Just as I believe God put Peter on that roof in Caesarea for a reason, I believe God put me in that 1920s home in Savannah for a reason. Perhaps at first, Peter didn't want to deal with the sins of the Gentiles. Maybe Peter preferred to keep the gospel to himself, like a wall separating him from the Gentiles. It would have been easy for me to think the same way at dinner with those two young women. But I refuse to hide my own beliefs to support the beliefs of others. I will not stop preaching the gospel just because someone is different than me. As believers, we are here to preach the message of love to the world. But before we can do that, we must deal with our own hearts first.

By facing your own heart first, you remember that you aren't called to judge, but you are called to love. You work through your own unbelief before you try and fix someone else's.

And yes, it's a fine line we walk when we share the gospel. While we are called to love everyone, we should never hint that there are many different ways to get to heaven. We can't preach a watered-down gospel. When God calls you to these conversations, you must remember not to run from them but be sympathetic to where people are in their faith journeys.

Why?

Because the gospel is for everyone. We have no right to determine who should and shouldn't hear the gospel. Like Peter was corrected in his vision before going to Cornelius, we, too, must correct ourselves first before sharing the gospel with others. If we don't, some of our experiences might end up as tragic as Gandhi's experience with Christianity.

While Gandhi was studying to be a lawyer in South Africa, he was given a Bible. He was absolutely captivated by what he read. In his intrigue, he decided to go to a Sunday service. He was met at the door by a leader with a confused look on his face. The leader looked him up and down and suggested he go to another church, one better suited for his kind.

Ghandi turned around and walked away. Not long after that encounter, he wrote about Christianity, "I like your Christ, I do not like your Christians. Your Christians are so unlike your Christ."

That's what happens when we go to Cornelius without fixing ourselves first. Our hearts must be fixed on the Savior first. Because if we're honest, our faith isn't summed up by our attendance on Sundays. It's not based on the steeples or the stained glass. Not the worship band or the production value. It's based on the honest hearts of a sinner in need of a Savior.

When God called Cornelius in the vision, He was calling him to Himself.

Like a perfectly laid plan, God then called Peter to cleanse his own heart first. And in classic Peter nature, he opened his mouth, which had proved troublesome in the past, what with Peter denying Jesus three times. But now, he was operating by the Holy Spirit.

God had called two people, and the Holy Spirit led them to one another. And in the end, Peter learned that God doesn't play favorites. He realized that there is no bigotry in the church or in the community of believers that God calls. Cornelius was baptized, and another follower entered the kingdom!

Day 11: Wall Destroyers

The God for Everyone

Sadly, the most segregated day of the week is still Sunday. We as people work together every weekday. We eat together, hang out together, laugh together, and live together. Yet, on Sundays, we worship separately.

Without a doubt, the Enemy is still working to separate us. He uses politics and culture to keep us from coming together. But God calls us to a different way. We must assimilate into the culture. Paul was able to be a Greek when around Greeks and a Jew when around the Jews. We must do the same and train ourselves to relate to different kinds of people, no matter how different they are from us.

Pastoral leader John Maxwell says, "Relationship-building is not the icing on the cake. It's the whole cake." When we get to know those who are different, those who are seemingly outcasts, those who appear unholy, that's when God can use us for his kingdom.

The modern-day hymn by the Getty's speak to the position of our hearts. Words that remind us to fix our own hearts before reaching others.

My soul is satisfied in Him alone
As summer flowers we fade and die
Fame, youth, and beauty hurry by
But life eternal calls to us
At the cross

I will not boast in wealth or might
Or human wisdom's fleeting light
But I will boast in knowing Christ
At the cross
[...]

The Revenant

Two wonders here that I confess
My worth and my unworthiness
My value fixed, my ransom paid
At the cross

And I rejoice in my Redeemer
Greatest Treasure, wellspring of my soul
And I will trust in Him, no other

May these words be helpful enough for your mind to understand the depth of God's love for *all* people. May they be convicting enough for you to turn inward on your own sin and prejudice. May they be encouraging enough for you to remember that your purpose here on Earth is not for pleasure or glory but for breaking down the walls that the Enemy builds, ones between people of different nationalities, different skin colors, different styles of worship, different denominations, different walks of life, different personalities. He's the God of everyone, so by the power of the Holy Spirit, let's destroy the Enemy's walls.

It's Not About *Me*, But *We*

Day 12

"Coming together is a beginning. Keeping together is progress. Working together is success."
Henry Ford

"When they heard these things they fell silent. And they glorified God, saying, 'Then to the Gentiles also God has granted repentance that leads to life.'"

Acts 11:18

As we just read in Acts 10, we read that Peter learned through a vision that the God he worships isn't just for the Jews. He is for *everyone*.

And in Acts 11, we read that Peter went to the apostles and explained his ministry to the Gentiles, providing evidence that the Lord wanted them to receive the Word of God. Conveniently, he seems to leave out the part where he, too, doubted the Lord when he was confronted about this controversy. But he does declare to the apostles, "If God gave the same gift to them as he gave us when we believed in the Lord Christ, who was I that I could stand in God's way?" (Acts 11:17).

You see, Peter's testimony to the apostles further affirmed God's plan all along. Jesus predicted it, the Holy Spirit gave witness to it, and Peter did too. This plan was never about one person but all people.

It's not about *me* but *we*.

This spiritual journey we're on, it's not for us to take alone. Rather, the Christian walk is meant to be done in tandem with other believers walking alongside us. There is power in numbers. There's predictability in persecution. There's strength in one another. But we must embrace each other to find it.

Power in a Cloud of Witnesses

When it comes to growing as a Christian, people debate whether or not personal testimonies or biblical knowledge are more effective. Does the knowledge and context of our religion help us to be better Christians? Of course. Does hearing a person's testimony help us understand Christ better? Of course.

In Acts 11, Peter gave evidence as to why his apostles should believe that Gentiles were filled with the Holy Spirit. It wasn't enough to tell them that they became believers in Christ. They had to understand why. And because of Peter's rich testimony, they reacted in stunned silence followed by glorifying the Lord. Their hearts were softened by Peter's story and ultimately overcome by God's Word.

While biblical knowledge gives way to a deeper connection to God, we also must understand why the Word is the Word. Someone's personal testimony goes far beyond what we say or declare. Why? Because there is immense power in a cloud of witnesses. There's immense power in the stories of one another

Day 12: It's Not About Me, But We

that are influenced by God. The writer of Hebrews tells us that "since we are surrounded by such a great cloud of witnesses, let us throw off everything that hinders the sin that so easily entangles" (Hebrews 12:1, NIV).

The truth is we all are a witness to someone else, and each of us is a witness of Jesus' love. Peter's testimony gave witness of Jesus working in the Gentiles. It further proved the spreading of the gospel throughout the world. And today, as Christians, we stand as witnesses of God in what we do and how we live.

There is a member of the church I'm currently pastoring that has quickly become my right-hand man. With an Italian Catholic background, he has zero knowledge of nondenominational worship—so much so, that I had to chuckle at a conversation we had about it the other day.

"Pastor Christian, I feel so out of place in worship. I'm looking around, and I see the hands in the air. But I just don't feel right asking questions in the middle of worship. I would love to meet with you one on one about questions I have, but why are so many people wanting to ask questions during the songs?"

It didn't take me long to piece together what he meant. I explained to him that they aren't raising their hands to ask questions, they are just moved by the Spirit so much so that they lift their hands to the Lord. His incredibly authentic comment was a breath of fresh air to me. This man—someone who brings many people to the church and gives freely—is not a seasoned member. He doesn't know much about church culture at all. He isn't corrupted at all by religion but is genuinely excited to learn more about Christ and be a witness to others around him.

This is what being a witness gives way to—an authentic love of God in others. To be a witness of Jesus means setting a godly example for other people in our lives. We do this by "throwing off" the sin that so easily tears us down. When we live this way,

The Revenant

other people will notice the proof of God's work in our lives, which is often much more powerful than simply knowing the Bible or being familiar with the church.

Once Peter finished sharing his testimony to the apostles, Acts 11:18 says they glorified God for more people had come to know Jesus. One man's testimony paved the way for many to grow in their faith.

The same goes for your own testimony. Your story is no small thing, and neither are the stories of Christians around you. There's power in your witnessing.

Persecution is Predictable

When a person tries to stomp out the embers of a fire, what happens?

It creates a draft and further fuels the fire. The small flames breathe into larger ones, extending like a blanket of heat all over the place. The same thing happened in the early church. As the good news spread, many tried to stomp it out by persecuting any Christian in sight. But as they did, the message just kept spreading and spreading, "to Jerusalem, Judea, Samaria, and the ends of the earth" (Acts 1:8). That was the theme of the gospel after all.

And God let Peter know that persecution was a part of the gig. Paul wrote that "Indeed, all who desire to live a godly life in Christ Jesus will be persecuted" (2 Timothy 3:12). Historically speaking, the church has generally grown during persecution. It doesn't grow when believers run away from suffering. On the contrary, the scattering of Christians did not occur because of fear, but because of excitement in the gospel! Peter understood that, and it led to a greater belief and confidence in what he was doing.

Day 12: It's Not About Me, But We

In the modern-day church, persecution works the same way. It *will* happen. It's a given when it comes to sharing the gospel. But it's nearly impossible to face alone. History shows this, and we must find encouragement in other believers as we live on this side of Eden.

In 1550, a man named Thomas Hawkes from England served as a page of the court for King Edward VI. When King Edward died, Catholics took over England, and protestants were in danger. After refraining from baptizing his son in the Catholic church, Hawkes was seen as unsound and became a prisoner in the Gatehouse of Westminster. After being given an ultimatum to convert to Catholicism, Hawkes stated that he would rather die than renounce his faith in the gospel.

While waiting to be put to death in prison, some other fellow believers asked if, when he was killed, he could lift his hands to show whether or not the pains were bearable. Hawkes replied, "by the help of God, to show them that the most terrible torments could be endured in the glorious cause of Christ and his gospel, the comforts of which were able to live the believing soul above all the injuries men could inflict."[4]

From there, Hawkes was fastened with chains to a stake and set on fire. As the flames encompassed his body and his skin melted and sizzled, most onlookers thought him dead. Then, out of nowhere, he lifted his hands, remembering his promise to his friends.

Hawkes let the believers know that suffering for Christ is worth the pain. It's part of our journey and many before us.

- James, brother of John, was beheaded.
- Thomas was stabbed with a spear.
- Simon, the brother of Jude, was crucified in Egypt.

---

[4] Nathan Johnson, "The Stirring Death Of Thomas Hawkes" *Deeper Christian*, accessed July 14, 2024, https://deeperchristian.com/thomas-hawke/.

The Revenant

- Simon the zealot was crucified.
- Mark was burned and buried after being drug through the streets.
- Bartholomew was beaten, skinned alive, and crucified. He still wouldn't die, so finally he was beheaded.
- Andrew was crucified.
- Matthew was run through with a spear.
- Philip was stoned and then crucified.
- James was thrown off the temple and continued to preach, so he was finally clubbed to death.
- Paul was beheaded.
- Luke, the author of Acts, was hanged upon an olive tree.
- Jude was shot to death by arrows.
- Mathias was stoned and then beheaded.
- Barnabas was stoned to death.
- Peter was crucified upside down.

If that's not enough, the only one who lived was John the Revelator. He was first boiled alive in oil but survived and was sentenced to work in a dark tunnel on the island of Patmos. In this miserable tunnel, with boils and blisters all over his body, he wrote the book of Revelation. Perhaps God had him write that book in the darkness with burns and blisters to convey that hell is a real place.

You see, God's greatest desire is to use our lives to reach the world. It's about the gospel coming to life in us. And it's unbearable to do this alone. Like Hawkes, Peter, and many before us, we, too, can lean on the testimonies and suffering of one another to get us through.

Day 12: It's Not About Me, But We

The People Behind the Legends

Most people know who Charles Lindberg was, but have you heard of Claude? Claude was Lindberg's mechanic that made the plane that would journey across the Atlantic for the very first time in history. Most people know of Martin Luther, but have you heard of Philip Melanchthon? He helped Luther translate the New Testament of the Bible. Many know of Billy Graham, but do you know T.W. and Grady Wilson? They cheered on Graham in his darkest moments of ministry.

Likewise, most people probably recognize the name Paul over Barnabas' name. Paul was a legend in the Bible, bringing many to Christ, writing a majority of the New Testament, and becoming a follower of Christ in the most unlikely of stories.

The truth is Barnabas isn't irrelevant in Paul's success.

In the last section of Acts 11, the gospel spreads to the city of Antioch through this guy named Barnabas. The city of Antioch was the second most important city in the Bible because that's where the Jews were dispersed after a great deal of persecution. If Rome was known for its power, Alexandria its intellect, and Athens its philosophy, then Antioch was known for its immorality.

Antioch was a city that was filled with prostitution and sin—perhaps the least likely of places for the gospel to spread. But as God's hand was on Peter and many before him, God's hand was also on Barnabas.

Barnabas was a good friend and source of encouragement for Saul. In Acts 9, Barnabas introduces Paul to the apostles who at first rejected him for his past life of persecuting Christians. Barnabas walked with him every step of the way and looked at Paul as the perfect weapon. He encouraged Paul in his struggle and reminded him that he was created for a purpose. And through the support and encouragement of Barnabas, Paul was recruited to teach all the nonbelievers about the gospel in Antioch.

You see, God creates all of us for a reason. And sometimes we need others to help us find it because it's not about *me* but about *we*.

Peace by Prayer

Day 13

"Peace comes not from the absence of trouble, but from the presence of God."
Alexander MacLaren

"So Peter was kept in prison, but earnest prayer for him was made to God by the church."

Acts 12:5

So far in our reading of the book of Acts, there has been great success in spreading the gospel. Many Jews and Gentiles alike came to know Christ. The Holy Spirit was on the move, and you could say things were going fairly well.

But in chapter 12, we read that James, one of Jesus' disciples, was killed with a sword. In fact, James was the very first disciple of Jesus to be martyred. And Peter? He wasn't safe either. Under the rule of Herod, Peter was imprisoned and would shortly be sentenced to death.

Much like the name Caesar, there are an abundance of Herods in history. Many of them have fought against God in pursuit of selfishness. The Herod in Acts chapter 12 was no different. This Herod was also called Agrippa I, and he was in the same family line as Herod the Great, who was called great only because of his building projects. He had ten wives and several kids—some of which he had murdered simply out of rage. In fact, on Herod the Great's deathbed, he had some innocent people executed just so people would be weeping at his funeral. Yep, that was his last act on earth, killing innocent people to make their community mourn at his death because he knew no one would cry over him.

Needless to say, Agrippa was the grandson of that evil man, and they were definitely similar in their harshness. He was friends with Emperor Caligula, a *really* bad Caesar. But Herod Agrippa I garnished favor with the Jews because he was circumcised. Jewish people loved him because he killed the Christians.

As you can imagine, the Jewish people celebrated Herod when James was killed. Upon James' death, Herod captured Peter and put him in jail—but not without an intense security detail. If you remember from earlier in Acts, some of the twelve had escaped from prison before, so Herod wasn't about to take that risk again. He put Peter under the watch of sixteen different soldiers, with four men rotating at a time. Of the four men on duty, two of them were chained to Peter and two were changing shifts.

All Herod had to do was wait to kill Peter because it was the Passover, and it was illegal to execute people over the Passover. (Jesus was killed during Passover because the prophecy had to be fulfilled.) If Herod killed Peter during the Passover, there would be a mob of angry Jews after him. Plus, he wanted to show all the Jews how perfectly he observed the Passover.

Day 13: Peace By Prayer

So Peter sat in jail chained to the guards just waiting to die. Unlike most of us if we were under the death sentence, though, Peter peacefully slept. Why? Because all through the night, the church was praying earnestly for him. As the great Puritan Thomas Watson wrote, "The angel fetched Peter out of prison, but prayer fetched the angel." You see, while Peter's gate was locked and his body chained, heaven's gate was opened wide by the power of prayer.

And if you didn't know it before, it's still a gate that's wide open for us too. Our prayers will always lead us to a Peter kind of peace.

A Peter Kind of Peace

While Peter sat peacefully in jail, an angel from heaven came upon him and threw off his chains. The passage reads:

> "Get up quickly" [the angel said]. And the chains fell off his hands. And the angel said to him, "Dress yourself and put on your sandals." And he did so. And he said to him, "Wrap your cloak around you and follow me." And he went out and followed him. He did not know if what was being done by the angel was real, but thought he saw a vision... When Peter came to himself, he said, "Now I am sure that the Lord has sent his angel and rescued me from the hand of Herod and from all that the Jewish people were expecting." (Acts 12: 7-9, 11)

You see, Peter thought he was having a vision at first, but with a heavenly nudge, he followed the angel out of jail and to Mary's house where everyone was praying for him.

That little nudge from heaven drew Peter out of his dark situation and led him into a home filled with peace.

Isn't it true that we all need a little nudge from the Lord in the midst of our tough situations? If I'm honest, sometimes nudges from the Lord feel more like punches from a collision with a Mac truck. After all, a relational woe, a cancer diagnosis, or a lost job are hardly small trials. But like Peter's moment in prison on death row, God uses even those dark moments to pull us toward peace.

As I'm pastoring this church in the Low Country of South Carolina, I recently met a young couple that just moved from Chicago. The young woman is recently divorced with a child, and the young man gave up med school to be with her. After attending the church for a couple of weeks, I got to know him a little bit more. I found out that not only is he very intelligent, but he is also a talented musician and plays the saxophone, drums, bass guitar, and sings like an angel. Excited, I asked him if he'd want to play in the worship band at church.

"Well," he stammered, "I'm not really a believer. Med school took it all out of me, but I like coming to church because of you." I was very uncomfortable with his response because *I'm* not the answer, but I knew he was on a journey and prayer was the best GPS (God's Positioning System) he could have to get there. So I prayed.

I smiled and they continued to come to church for a few more weeks after getting a house together in the Savannah area. Unfortunately, things did not work out with his girlfriend. She ended up leaving him shortly thereafter for her ex-husband, and this dark situation left him shattered.

The hope and happiness he once exuded were now drained, and he was quickly whisked into a depression that made him want to kill himself. I drove over to his house and hugged his tired body.

"Right now," I told him, "you feel alone in the world and like nothing can get better from here. But what if this dark moment in

Day 13: Peace By Prayer

your life is actually a nudge from God, leading you to where you're supposed to be? See, sometimes nudges come in disappointment. Heartbreak. Uprooting. But God can use even those moments to lead you to peace. God has broken you down to rebuild you," I added, "if you let Him."

A week later, he came to church on a Wednesday night. I had taken off that particular day, and it so happened that this brilliant Messianic Jew was speaking that night. He was talking about Daniel 9 and how it proved that the coming of Jesus was predicted in Jerusalem. In fact, it was predicted to the month *and* day that He would be crucified! That night, this young man gave his life to Christ. God took me out of the way and brought the exact voice and message he needed to hear and the way he needed to hear it and a life was transformed. He went from a place of hurt, frustration, and hopelessness to a place of complete peace. And it all came through prayer.

God went so far as to take away the person that this man loved most, all to reach his heart. And now my brother in Christ is resting in the Lord with a Peter kind of peace. He is doing much better, and who knows? Maybe he will be a worship pastor one day.

But what's true is that the Lord will take just as great measures for you too. It's up to you to be sensitive to His nudges and trust that His path for you will lead to peace.

Prayer Changes Things

I'm sure that somewhere in our country in a principal's office hangs a sign that reads, *In case of nuclear attack, earthquake, or fire, the ban on prayer will be temporarily lifted.*

Why?

Because when the going gets tough, the tough get praying. Even nonbelievers resort to praying as a last-ditch effort. In our most desperate times of need, we pray diligently for help.

As the passage says, the church kept praying for Peter as he was in jail. They diligently prayed that God would protect Peter and make a way for him. Lo and behold, God intervened. He helped Peter escape from prison unscathed, and that's because prayer changes circumstances.

Well, except when it doesn't. I mean, think about it. I'm sure that when James was killed with the sword, the disciples wondered why God didn't save him. Did they not pray for James? Did they not diligently ask God to save him as they did Peter? Of course, they did. Like with Peter, God heard their prayers for James and He answered them.

Only his answer was, well, *no*.

God tells us that His thoughts are higher than our thoughts and that His ways are higher than our ways (Isaiah 55:8). And at that moment, the disciples had to trust that His promise was true. That they would not leave the earth until the Lord willed it so. This kind of trust is why they could live so carefreely for the gospel. Because they knew that in the end, God was the one with the final say.

While our prayers don't always amount to exactly what we think they should, they *always* make a difference. Each one of our life stories is influenced by our prayers and the prayers from others made on our behalf. But at the end of the day, God makes the final call. In other words, God has final "editing rights" to our unique stories. He knows the path that our stories should take to bring glory to the kingdom.

My question to you is are your prayers proof of your trust in God? In the midst of conflict in your church, are you pursuing God's heart by praying for peace above all things? Through

Day 13: Peace By Prayer

infidelity in your marriage, are you praying that God's will be done above your will? With a wayward child, are you praying that God reaches your child in a way only He can?

In your prayers, are you trusting God's answer above your own?

Peter trusted that path as he sat chained in prison. He trusted the Lord when the angel woke him up from his peaceful slumber. Like Peter, we must rest on God's promises while we're in the land of the living. He trusted God's promises as he continued to spread the good news to the Jews and the Gentiles. Bottom line, Peter trusted. And I can't help but wonder if his radical trust had something to do with persistent prayer.

Because, friend, prayer changes things.

Like English hymn writer William Cowper once said, "Satan trembles when he sees the weakest Christian on his knees."

Even in our weakest, most vulnerable moments, our prayers matter. When we send our prayers to our God, we can be sure that while our exact circumstances may not change, our hearts will. Through prayer, God aligns our hearts with His own, making us rest in the peace of His will.

His good and pleasing and perfect will.

"Trust in the LORD forever, for the LORD, the LORD himself, is the Rock eternal" (Isaiah 26:4, NIV).

To Be Called Christian

Day 14

"The name that's lifted up forever, the name that shakes the earth and shakes the heavens, the hope for every heart, the Savior of the world, Jesus, Jesus."

Jesus Culture

"And we bring to you the good news that what God promised to the fathers, this he has fulfilled to us their children by raising Jesus, as also it is written in the second Psalm,

'You are my Son, today I have begotten you.'"

Acts 13:32-33

You'll remember we learned about Barnabas in chapter 11 when he brought Saul to Antioch. It was because of the strong friendship of Barnabas that Saul preached the Word of God to nonbelievers in corrupt Antioch. It was also in Antioch that followers of Christ were no longer called people of the Way but were called Christians.

Day 14: To Be Called Christian

There's a whole lot of power in that name we share: Christian.

My mother was very intentional and adamant naming me Christian. She never wanted anyone to call me Chris because my name was Christian. After all, it means follower of Christ—the most important thing about me. One day, I was playing golf with an older gentleman I had just met. He kept referring to me as Chris.

"Alright, Chris, you're up. Nice swing, Chris! Good shot, Chris."

Eventually, I had to speak up. "Hey, brother, I have to let you know that I'd like you to call me Christian not Chris. My name is Christian. Do you know what Christian means?"

He replied, "No, what does it mean?"

"It means follower of Christ, and do you know what Chris means?"

"No, what?"

"Nothing, so please call me Christian." He laughed and called me Christian for the rest of our day because he knew it was a strong conviction of my heart.

I chuckle when I tell this story, but there is a lot of truth to it. When we are in Christ, we are a new creation. We adopt that valuable name Christian, and it becomes the most important thing about us.

Because bigger than any nickname or any family name is the name that has bound us together for centuries. It's the name that is our past, present, and future. It's where we come from and where we're going.

A Narrative of the Two Thieves

Acts 13 shows us the very first organized effort of missions. Before that, Christians would be sent out by the Holy Spirit to spread the Word of God throughout the region. But now, the church was supporting them and sending them out. Members

The Revenant

of the congregation would pray and fast for these missionaries, believing that God would be with them. With a powerful sendoff, Paul and Barnabas set out for Cyprus. John Mark—the same Mark who later wrote the Gospel of Mark—traveled with them as an assistant. He was incredibly helpful to Paul and Barnabas because he was an eyewitness of Jesus' ministry.

It's important to understand that like us, early missionaries were separated *to* God, meaning they were called to specific good work by the Holy Spirit. They had to separate from what they knew—from a life of comfort and safety—to fulfill God's call. Paul would later write, "For we are his workmanship, created in Christ Jesus for good works, which God prepared beforehand that we should walk in them" (Ephesians 2:10). As Christians, Paul and Barnabas had to cling to the Holy Spirit to lead them in the way.

It's a mysterious and powerful thing, the Holy Spirit. Sometimes in a whisper and other times in a loud shout, He beckons us closer to Jesus.

In college, a pastor from a local church discipled me. I was playing baseball and studying to be a Wesleyan pastor at the time. We often met and discussed how to live an expressive life for Christ, and I was growing closer to that each day. One day, he asked me to preach at the college ministry where there would be close to five hundred students! That was *huge* for me!

On the bus to our next baseball game, the team chatted and goofed around in the seats while I sat alone in the chair preparing my sermon. As I pondered a compelling topic, the Holy Spirit kept softly prompting me in that still, small voice. He kept pressing me to talk about the two thieves next to Jesus on the cross (Luke 23:39-43).

The Spirit impressed upon me to name them.

Day 14: To Be Called Christian

You see, the Bible doesn't tell us the names of these thieves. We knew their criminal life, but apart from that, nothing.

"Name them. Tell their stories," the Spirit whispered.

For the remainder of the bus ride, I made up this entirely dramatic story of these two thieves leading up to the cross. Like the Holy Spirit instructed, I named them. One was named Aaron, which means "strong-willed." I imagined Aaron to be stubborn and firm because of his mountainous strength. The other thief I named Joshua, which means "God is my deliverance." These two boys grew up as best friends in a small town. Their parents had dreams for them to grow up to be God-fearing Jews, perhaps even Rabbis! However, the boys soon started rebelling against their parents and lived in a way that did not please them. Eventually, their parents had to cut them loose.

Not too long after their parents let them go, I imagined they got caught robbing a home. They were set to be crucified with Jesus the next day. Now, Joshua received paradise because he humbled himself and received the message of grace. But Aaron did not. Because of Aaron's strong-willed spirit, he stubbornly and pridefully rejected the gospel.

I literally told this entire narrative for thirty minutes to five hundred college students. At the end of the story, I preached to them how they, too, could receive paradise and grace. I reminded them not to reject the gospel like Aaron, and to be soft to the nudge of the Holy Spirit. From there, I went into an altar call.

What happened next, I never expected.

Absolutely nothing.

No one came down to the altar.

I felt like a complete failure. My very first sermon—one for which I thought that the Holy Spirit very clearly prepped me— yielded zero responses. Describing myself as being embarrassed would be an understatement.

The Revenant

As the night ended and students headed home, a college kid came up to me and said, "Christian, tonight I gave my life to Jesus."

Stunned, I shook his hand and asked him why he didn't raise his hand or come down the altar.

"Well, I struggle with pride and when you told that story about stubborn and prideful Aaron, I really related to that. I knew that his story was mine."

Overjoyed, I embraced him. "This is great news, man. What's your name?" I asked.

He responded, "My name is Aaron."

Who We Are

From Cyprus to the island of Paphos, Paul and Barnabas traveled and shared the gospel with the people. In Paphos, they encountered opposition in the form of a Jewish magician who referred to himself as Elymas, but his real name was Bar-Jesus, meaning "son of Jesus," which Paul and Barnabas refused to call him.

This Jewish magician was well-rounded and picked up culture wherever he went. He accumulated a variety of religions and was not living out his Jewish background. Filled with the Holy Spirit, Paul confronted Elymas, and he was blinded. I can't help but wonder if Paul recalled his own first encounter with the Holy Spirit when he, too, was blinded. Maybe when you lose your own identity and name, it's better to be blind. Because only then can you see where your real identity is—inside.

Our identities are not anchored in where we were born or in what religion we were raised. We are not what we accomplish or how many friends we have. Identity has nothing to do with followers on Twitter or the number of people in your church

Day 14: To Be Called Christian

ministry. Our identity is anchored firmly in Jesus Christ, from whom we get our name: Christian.

Paul and Barnabas clung tightly to their Christian identity. And from there, the Holy Spirit did the rest of the work throughout the regions.

Once leaving Paphos, Barnabas and Paul traveled to Perga. From then on Luke no longer refers to them as "Paul and Barnabas" but as "Paul and his party." This shows the great prominence and leadership Paul had as a missionary of Christ. God used his strength to spread His Word to the nations.

After Perga, Paul and his party set sail to Antioch in Pisidia where Paul was given a customary invitation to speak at the synagogue. Happily, Paul took this opportunity to explain Israel's detailed and rich history that points so beautifully to Jesus. His sermon touched on the holy events God planned, from leading His people out of Egypt to Jesus' burial and resurrection and everything in between.

Paul said boldly, "Let it be known to you, therefore, brothers, that through this man forgiveness of sins is proclaimed to you, and by him everyone who believes is freed from everything from which you could not be freed by the law of Moses" (Acts 13:38-39).

Each and every event that Paul described pointed to the mighty name that we carry with us today: JESUS.

And the crowds? They were in absolute awe. The response to Paul and Barnabas was great, and this filled the missionaries with joy and confidence. However, the very next Sabbath, the Jews were "filled with jealousy and began to contradict what was spoken by Paul, reviling him. And Paul and Barnabas spoke out boldly, saying, 'It was necessary that the word of God be spoken first to you. Since you thrust it aside and judge yourselves so unworthy of eternal life, behold we are turning to the Gentiles . . .

the word of the Lord was spreading throughout the whole region' " (Acts 13:45-46, 49). In a matter of one short week, the perceptions of Barnabas and Paul were drastically changed. People went from rejoicing in the synagogue to persecuting the pair of bold missionaries.

At the same time, in this one short week, the church was born. Those receptive to the gospel rejoiced in God and formed a church, spreading the Good News to the region. And those who responded with hostility stirred up persecution against Paul and Barnabas. Like the thief Aaron (from my story), some were too strong-willed and prideful to accept the good news from God through Paul's party.

The dramatic events that ensued after preaching the gospel came as no surprise to Paul or Barnabas. They knew by now that to be called a Christian sometimes meant tribulation. They knew to be called Christian often meant being questioned. And they knew to be called Christian meant a life of courage by the power of the Holy Spirit.

Paul and Barnabas's very names reminded them of their true identity: Christians.

Followers of Jesus from the beginning of time to the end of eternity. It's who they are. And it's who we are today too, if you are a follower of Christ.

Pride's Antidote

Day 15

*"Humility is not thinking less of yourself,
it is thinking of yourself less."*

C.S. Lewis

"Men, why are you doing these things? We also are men, of like nature with you, and we bring you good news, that you should turn from these vain things to a living God, who made the heaven and earth and the sea and all that is in them."

Acts 14:15

While the good news of the gospel hasn't changed over the centuries, our approach in spreading it has. Today, many pastors share the gospel from stages, arenas, and coffeehouses. Some preach in suits and others preach in T-shirts. And all too often, pride gets in the way of which approach is the "better" way, the "more righteous" way, the "right" way.

Pride.

It's a word that isolates many people from the faith and creates exclusive circles of people within the faith. And it's probably the biggest contender in things that prevent the spread of the gospel.

In Mark 1, the Greek word *euanggelion* is translated as *gospel* and means "good news." The gospel means good news. But if we're not careful, the good news can easily become bad news by the way we present and communicate it. When we live out prideful actions and words, that good news is lost on many who need to hear it.

What's the antidote for such a thing? Humility. It negates our pride and reminds us of our need for Christ. Without humility, we have no chance of sharing the right gospel.

In Acts 14, Paul and Barnabas found themselves in a tempting situation—one that enticed their pride and flattered their accomplishments. After preaching in Lystra, the crowds looked to Paul and Barnabas as though they were Greek gods. Paul was looked upon as Hermes, the chief speaker, and Barnabas was admired as Zeus due to his strong authority. These apostles had a chance to accept this flattery and own the miracles the Lord was doing through them.

But they had a spirit stronger than that. Paul and Barnabas knew the value of humility because they knew a God greater than Zeus and Hermes. Their God created all things and sustains all things.

See, these apostles understood the vastness of the one true God. They clung to the cross where He was crucified. They believed in the teachings of Jesus that directed their every word. As a result, Paul and Barnabas rejected any level of praise they were given by the crowds because they knew it was undeserved.

If the crowd saw greatness, it would only attest to the true author and perfector of our faith. Let's take a look at their journey.

Where Humility Comes From

During Paul's first missionary journey, when Paul and Barnabas reached Iconium, they encountered great opposition, which they were used to. They decided not to leave the place until absolutely necessary in order to spread the gospel as far as possible. While in Iconium they preached boldly, trusting in the God they knew directed their steps. Just as Jesus spoke lovingly and gracefully to the woman at the well in Samaria, Paul spoke to the people's needs in Iconium. He preached about God's grace, a grace that was enough for both the Jews and the Gentiles. At this notion, Paul and Barnabas were about to be stoned, so they left for Lystra and Derbe to continue their mission of the Lord.

While in Lystra, they healed a crippled man. The crowd of people was so astonished they began worshiping Paul and Barnabas for their "healing powers."

As ministry leaders, Christian mentors, or discipleship partners, there's a risk of nonbelievers looking at us as "more holy" just as they did with Paul and Barnabas. And if we're not careful about checking the postures of our hearts, there's a risk we might accept that flattery and bask in the glory that others give us. With prideful hearts, our actions can quickly go rogue. We might start lacing our prayers with elegant language to get admirers. Or fill our messages with anecdotes of our greatness to make us look righteous. Perhaps we might start viewing worship time as a performance for all the fans who look our way. I know it sounds drastic, but when we forget to check our hearts, they so quickly turn to pride. Humility is the less natural posture—the one that is contingent upon understanding our great need.

Thankfully, Paul and Barnabas had the humility to decline the adoration they received from the crowds. Their humility is what continued the message and zeal of the gospel. See, once these apostles were given the praise and admiration from the crowds, they tore their clothes to prove they were not gods, but completely human. They begged the crowds to "turn from these useless things," referring to the idolatry of the people.

You see, the message of Paul and Barnabas always went straight to the cross at Calvary. It never once tiptoed around God's grace and power. And that, believer, is where the heart of humility starts. It begins with knowing that everything we have starts at the cross. Charles Spurgeon knew that. This famous preacher would say that he'd take the Scripture and make a beeline to the cross. He knew that without the cross, all was lost and nothing else mattered.

The Jesus Storybook Bible: Every Story Whispers His Name is a great example of how Jesus is the center of every story in the Old Testament. The authors wrote this children's Bible to point to the work of Jesus. Through Adam and Eve, Jesus' name is figuratively whispered as a true and better Adam. In the story of Ruth and Naomi, it was Boaz who was the Redeemer. The story points to Jesus, the *greater* Redeemer. Through the story of Abraham sacrificing Isaac, we hear a whisper of Jesus being the true sacrificial Son.

While it's easy to preach about Old Testament messages for the story, what's the use if it doesn't connect back to Jesus? What is the reason for telling the story of David, Moses, or Noah without understanding that *Jesus* is the greater David, Moses, and Noah? Our humility takes root at the feet of Jesus.

Think about what could change if we viewed the world through the eyes of humility. How would our parenting change when our kids mess up? How would our marriages change when our spouse does something disappointing? How would our ministries change when volunteers or staff members did something frustrating?

Day 15: Pride's Antidote

Those things would change immensely because our hearts as Christians should live in a constant posture of humility. When that's the case, our message will always point to Calvary. It will begin and end with our need for Jesus, and what He did for us to be with Him forever.

Spurgeon understood that. He would always end up at the cross because he knew that's what it was all about. There is only success in Christ and his grace. When we pursue other titles and accomplishments, they always fall short.

Jesus is both our confidence and our humility.

My Doors are Open

Once Paul and Barnabas declined the invitation to be worshiped like gods, the crowds turned on them. Like they turned on him in Iconium, the crowds in Lystra stoned Paul and dragged him out of the city. Everyone wished him dead, and honestly, everyone thought he was dead too. But when the disciples—his church—gathered around him, he rose and went back to preaching! I can't imagine what the crowds thought when they saw Paul rise up and continue spreading the gospel. Without a doubt, Paul's zeal for Jesus had to have made a major impact on their lives.

In the shadow of Christ, we're humbled. Our work is useless without Him. After high school I got married, and my wife, Amy, and I moved into a small house outside of our college in South Carolina. As a baseball player, I was friends with many of the athletes at our school, and my wife became friends with some of them too.

Rachel played volleyball and really connected with Amy, and I was friends with her boyfriend at the time. As their relationship developed, Rachel and her boyfriend engaged in premarital sex.

She got pregnant and her boyfriend then wanted nothing to do with her.

The consequences of the pregnancy created many differences in their lives. The school found out, but Rachel was the only one who was shamed. She lost her scholarship for the year. She was told to have the baby and return to finish the rest of the year.

In the midst of this situation, Amy and I ached for Rachel and her new baby. We let her move into our small home until she gave birth to her sweet baby, Melissa. That year, I graduated and was pastoring at a ministry called DCF (Downtown Community Fellowship) in Clemson, South Carolina. Amy and I would help take care of baby Melissa so Rachel could finish the rest of her school year.

Looking back on that situation, I would do it all over again. We weren't trying to earn anything or get anything from Rachel by letting her live with us. We were simply living out the Scriptures. Amy and I were no better than Rachel, and we knew how important it was for us to help her. Just as we would hope someone would do the same thing for us if we were in that situation, we chose to serve her and show her the grace of the Lord as best we could. Through our humble perspectives, it was clear that God was telling us that we, too, could have been in the same situation. We all need help sometimes. How could I ever assume I'm better than Rachel?

The only response we could show was compassion. Not because we were compassionate on our own, but because God showed us the same compassion. It only made sense to pay it forward.

Years later, Rachel married an amazing, godly man. They had several kids together, and she now serves as a worship leader in Sumter, South Carolina. Well, one Sunday while preaching at my church I see a familiar man in the congregation with two children. After the service, Amy and I approached the family to introduce ourselves.

The man shook our hands and introduced himself as Brandon, and my wife immediately recognized his face.

"Wait, you are Rachel's son! And you're Rachel's husband!"

It turned out that Rachel's son was starting college right by our church, and he was going to start attending! It was truly a full-circle moment for me and Amy. One that would have never happened if we would have treated Rachel the way the school did all those years ago. Instead of pushing her out and rejecting her because of her pregnancy, we loved her. We opened our home to her. We didn't view ourselves as more righteous but saw the same humanity in Rachel that we had.

I don't tell this story to boast but to remind you that when you decrease yourself, you see others with the eyes of Christ.

As we chatted with Rachel's family, her son turned to us and said, "Thank you for loving my mom."

I don't remember my response. But I do remember what I thought.

"Thank you, God, for loving me."

That is where it all starts.

The Majors and Minors of Faith

Day 16

"When it comes to entities that God has created specifically to make disciples and accomplish His mission, there is the church... and nothing else."

Reggie Joiner

"And there arose a sharp disagreement, so that they separated from each other. Barnabas took Mark with him and sailed away to Cyprus, but Paul chose Silas and departed, having been commended by the brothers to the grace of the Lord."

Acts 15:39-40

There have been many moments in my personal life and in ministry where I've gotten into a disagreement with someone. You know how that feels.

Someone says something ignorant, and the comment hits you like a sharp arrow to the brain. Your own ideas and opinions start to bubble up, and eventually they spew out like a shaken Coke bottle. Sometimes in a harsh way, other times in a more

Day 16: The Majors And Minors Of Faith

reserved way, but regardless of how your opinions flow out of your mouth, the point is that they *do* flow out.

Chick-fil-A is hands down better than Zaxby's.

Marvel is better than DC.

Dogs over cats.

Netflix over Amazon Prime.

Political red over blue.

Some of these superficial statements can start quite a heated debate depending on who's in the room. Trust me, I know that it takes great strength to let other people go on believing in their incorrect opinions—especially when it comes to food! But at the end of the day, you and I both know it doesn't actually matter what someone's opinions are. These silly things are simply not worth fighting about.

If you're in a relationship or are married, you know one of the best pieces of advice is to pick your battles. If you make a big deal of everything, nothing is a big deal.

But as Christians, the topic of salvation is certainly a big deal and one that is worth fighting for. In Acts 15, we will see just how important the gospel is to Paul and Barnabas. So important, in fact, that it would eventually drive them apart.

What's Worth Fighting For?

It's clear that all humans experience disagreement. Walter Martin, a Baptist minister and founder of Bible Answer Man, said it best: "If you can find two people agreeing on everything, someone is not thinking." Sometimes, we are called to contend and put up a good fight for the faith. It happened in the Old Testament all the time.

Jacob had a disagreement with his Uncle Laban which led to a separation between them. Abraham and Lot decided to separate due to a disagreement among the shepherds. The disciples had a disagreement over who was the most important in the kingdom of heaven. We have a long history of separation due to a division of beliefs. But the importance is to distinguish what is truly worth separating over.

I've been a church planter for many years now. I learned from a successful church planter and mentor, John Reeves. He would put a church anywhere except a gas station. He and his wife started a church at a Ramada Hotel bar! After growing out of the bar area, he moved to an Esso Bar and Grill across from Clemson's football stadium, Death Valley. Once it outgrew the bar and grill, he moved the church to a printing warehouse, where it continued to grow and grow. It seemed every Sunday, someone was walking up the dike with several college students to Lake Hartwell for baptisms. The church went from one Sunday service to an additional Saturday night service, to three services on Saturday night and two on Sunday! At its height of success, close to one thousand college students were coming to hear the gospel each week. And it all started with a couple of people at the little hotel bar.

Throughout this process of church planting and growing, we had zero disagreements over the small, unimportant things. We majored in the majors and minored in the minors. And while we were all very different, we came together and did great work for Christ.

Not all church planting experiences go as smoothly as this one, though. I led another church rebuild where leaders of the church were making huge deals over small things. And like we mentioned before, some things—like Zaxby's and Chick-fil-A—are simply not worth fighting over.

After the COVID-19 pandemic, I resigned from the church where I had been serving for twenty years and moved to the low

Day 16: The Majors And Minors Of Faith

country of South Carolina to help rebuild a church. For years, I had been trained to plant churches and had seen success in that area of ministry but felt called to rebuild a church that needed growth. I mean, think about how many churches in America have a building, land, and a growing community but don't have anyone prepared to take the gospel to those in need.

So, my wife and I prayed and were led by God to a church of fifteen people in the middle of a bursting community. Upon arrival it was clear to me many of the growth issues they were having were due to majoring in the minors and minoring in the majors. It was brought to my attention that some people were concerned about me and my family not being vaccinated. I noticed that there was tension because of my conservative views when I made it perfectly clear that politics didn't belong in the church, but only the gospel message of Jesus. There was often trivial conversation about the facilities—what doors remained open or closed, lights stayed on or off, who had the keys to the building and forgot to lock the door. All of these conversations were replacing the needed conversation about the homeless in our community, those battling sickness, and how to get the gospel out to the lost. They were baffled by my approach of not doing office hours at the church but rather riding around town on my Onewheel electric skateboard all day meeting new people and sharing God's love with strangers.

These minor issues were passionately addressed by me because they had a *major* effect on the growth of the church, which ultimately affects the spread of the gospel. Focusing on the minors and forgetting to address the majors is nothing new but rather an issue in the church as old as time.

In Acts 15, Paul and Barnabas fought the people of Judea over serious matters of salvation—about whether or not Gentiles had to be circumcised to be saved. It was a matter they would not back down on, and one in which God proved to have the final say. As the modern church, we know that we will experience disagreements, but it is most important that these disagreements are about something serious, something worth fighting over.

After Paul and Barnabas returned to Antioch to tell the Gentiles that they were saved by grace alone through faith alone, another disagreement popped up. Only this time, it was between the two of them. While we don't know exactly what their disagreement was about, we know it had to do with whether or not to take John Mark with them. Barnabas wanted to take him, but Paul did not. Neither apostle would back down on this minor issue, and it led to separation.

Disagreements bring out the humanity in all of us. Sometimes, the greatest disciples in the world will disagree with each other. But as a church, you must decide what is truly relevant. What topics of contempt *should* get in the way of our unity?

Over the years, I have had to consistently show love and grace, but also grit and passion for the integrity of the gospel. I was not willing to back down or give way to tradition but rather have been willing to fight for every family, not just in the church but for the families that God would eventually bring our way. For me, the church and the gospel is worth fighting for.

Though we can't claim megachurch status, I can say that our church has gone from fifteen attending Sunday worship service to over one hundred. We have gone from having no children to having a thriving children's ministry. From no youth or college students to a healthy gathering of young people from local high schools and colleges. From no life groups to five healthy ones gathering in our community. From $2,500 in tithes and offerings to close to $15,000 each month. These are some of

Day 16: The Majors And Minors Of Faith

the benefits that occur when a church focuses on the majors and not the minors.

You Can't Stitch What's Already Been Torn

When churches try to preach a different gospel, tweaking it enough just to highlight their hand-picked issues, division is sure to happen. Paul addressed the Galatian church, warning them about how they can fall away from God. He reminded them how dangerous it is to mix God's grace and the law like oil and water.

When Paul and Barnabas excitedly shared with the Gentiles that they can be saved without circumcision, many Jews strongly disagreed with God's Word. I mean, they were basically majoring on the minors. But Paul and Barnabas stood firm in their disagreement because this one was huge. Salvation always is.

See, when you try to use the law to offset God's grace, it's like stitching back up the veil that was already torn. The Temple veil that was ripped in two when Jesus died was woven with motifs directly from the loom. Each curtain had the thickness of a handbreadth or about four fingers wide. It was impossible for any man to rip it in his own strength. Only God could have torn the veil. And when he did, it tore from top to bottom. This veil that separated the Holy of Holies from the rest of the temple signified how men were separated from God by sin. But when Jesus died, the veil tore, signifying how we may now enter God's presence. The debt was paid. It is finished.

And if it is truly finished, why on earth would we try to add to it?

That would be like me adding to Michelangelo's painting in the Sistine Chapel. You can't even take flash photography in the chapel to preserve the masterpiece. Why would I ever attempt to make this work of art better?

The Revenant

It would be like me adding to Beethoven's Symphony No. 5. The genius composer would dump his head in freezing water just to stay alert so he wouldn't lose creativity. How could I ever understand the depth of this composition to add to it?

Or perhaps it would be like me adding to Edgar Allen Poe's famous 1849 poem *A Dream Within a Dream*. In the midst of suffering from alcoholism, Poe wrote this dark and moving poem that touched millions. How could I ever add any word to that masterpiece to enhance it?

Before Jesus died, the Torah had 613 commandments to follow. Of those 613 commandments, 248 were positive. That leaves 365 thou shalt nots, enough for one each day of the year! There were twenty-four chapters alone on how to keep the Sabbath, going as far as to tell you how much weight you can carry on a Sabbath day! The laws were unrealistic to follow and remember. (I mean, you had to make sure it wasn't unlawful to pick up a fig for goodness' sake.) That's the thing about the law. It's always more negative than positive. But Paul and Barnabas preached that by faith through God's grace we can live in freedom from the law. And this truth was the one they'd stand by no matter the obstacles in their way.

The leaders in history and in the modern church who majored on the minors are like the yoke that would chafe the oxen raw. Why would anyone want such pain to continue? In the same way, we have to *choose* a life of freedom, *clinging* to the grace God gave us when the veil was torn.

Our freedom has long been established in Christ. In Him, we have freedom from the petty asks of the law. We need not stitch back the veil that God has ripped; we need only celebrate the freedom He's gifted us.

Disagreements will come. And when they do, let's choose to stand up for the ones that truly matter and let the minor issues

Day 16: The Majors And Minors Of Faith

go. Why? Because this work we're doing for Christ is a finished work. Let it stay finished.

Stops and Steps

DAY 17

"It's an obvious by vital truth: Without God's leading, we go our own way."
Chuck Swindoll

"Paul wanted Timothy to accompany him, and he took him and circumcised him because of the Jews who were in those places, for they all know that his father was a Greek. As they went on their way through the cities, they delivered to them for observance the decisions that had been reached by the apostles and elders who were in Jerusalem. So the churches were strengthened in the faith, and they increased in numbers daily."

Acts 16:3-5

A few years back when I was an itinerant pastor, I was asked to speak at a church in an extremely small town in Georgia. The church sat between a family-owned bank and a Mennonite restaurant, across from the only light and gas station in town. It's the kind of small town you see in movies. And boy, it was

Day 17: Stops And Steps

different than what I was accustomed to. At the time, my type of gig was large churches in populated cities. Compared to the fast-paced environment I was used to, this church assignment felt like a slam on the breaks.

That night, I found myself wide awake around midnight in that little town. I decided to get out of bed and planted myself at a crossroads for several hours watching the stoplight turn from green to yellow to red. The crickets chirped, the lightning bugs lit up the nighttime landscape, and the stars illuminated the heavens.

To this day, I have never felt a moment more peaceful than that. As I watched the light change colors, I was reminded of the churches where I usually preached. I reflected on where I was in the present moment—this small, unassuming town in Georgia. *Maybe God,* I thought, *was telling me to stop and slow down.*

It took me going to the middle of nowhere to realize that God's leading can come in green, yellow, and red lights. All paces play an important role in His plan. The stops are just as important as the steps.

In Acts 16, the Lord led Paul to a certain disciple named Timothy. And at the perfect time, no less. John, Mark and Barnabas had just separated from Paul and God provided Timothy to go on with him. In their travels together, the Lord led them in a straight line to their destination. The winds were at their back, allowing the disciples to make good time to deliver the good news of the gospel to the crowds. It's as though God gave them every green light and made their journey as efficient as possible.

But later, on their way to Rome, the wind went against them. Yellow lights slowed down their journey, giving them some struggles and even some red-light obstacles. As Paul and Timothy experienced green, yellow, and red lights while following God, our own lives can play out in the same way. When we follow our own desires, we often find ourselves zig-zagging and floundering along the path. But like Paul and Timothy, when we follow the Lord, we're taken in a straight line.

And while there won't always be green lights at every intersection, God's stops often lead to mighty steps.

Whatever It Takes

While on their missions around the world, Paul continued being adamant that uncircumcised Gentiles could be saved and stood up against legalism. His biggest passion was to remind the crowds that God's grace was enough, and salvation can be theirs by simply believing in the Lord as Christ!

But then Paul had Timothy circumcised.

I know what you're thinking. Isn't this a complete contradiction of what Paul preached all this time? Aren't we supposed to let go of legalistic practices like this? Yes and also no.

I do agree that it does, at first glance, seem like Paul abandoned his original stance by having Timothy give into the practices of the law. On the contrary, Paul still fully believed that salvation comes by faith alone through grace alone. Grace is enough, period. Here's the important part: Paul's passion for the gospel to be spread was so great, so passionate, so important that he didn't want *anything* to get in the way of it spreading to the Jews of that region.

You see, Timothy *had* to get circumcised. If not, these Jews would immediately shut the disciples down without giving them a second look. And Timothy? He, too, felt so strongly about the spread of the gospel that he didn't even argue about circumcision. He did it willingly (and you men know this was

Day 17: Stops And Steps

no easy ask. There were no meds to numb the pain, and no efficient utensils to get it done quickly or cleanly. There was just a sharp rock to do the job!) That's just how much Timothy loved the gospel.

Paul and Timothy would do whatever it took to tell people about the Lord. Even if it took some painful red lights along the way.

I wish I understood this as a young pastor. Shockingly, I was asked to speak at my childhood church after becoming a pastor. If you remember, my childhood church was an extremely traditional Wesleyan church in Kannapolis, North Carolina. Gone were the days when I felt I had to wear a suit on a Sunday or recite the Apostles' Creed from memory. Quite frankly, I wanted to make a point about how much I didn't feel convicted to do those things anymore.

The Sunday I spoke I wore my casual clothes just to make a point. I walked up to the podium proudly and preached my heart out, hoping the congregation would finally realize how ridiculous their legalistic beliefs were. After the message, it was clear no one listened to me. No one asked any questions. No one even seemed a bit engaged or took me seriously. I was both incredibly annoyed and embarrassed by that.

Afterward, I called my mentor and vented to him on the phone. "Man, these people are so cold and stuck in legalism. I'm sure if I wore a suit, they would have listened to me."

"Well, if that's what it takes to make the gospel go forward, why wouldn't you wear a suit?"

At that moment, I realized that some battles truly are worth fighting for. Salvation is always worth the fight. From then on, I made a point to call the head pastor of where I'm speaking and get a read on the congregation. What are the people going through? How long are the typical sermons? What is the dress code? What version of the Bible is used? To this day, I find out what the church needs to be able to *hear* my message.

Why would I let such small things get in the way of people hearing the gospel? This was exactly Paul and Timothy's mentality. If they could help it, they wouldn't let a pesky red light get in the way of their journey. They used each stop to make an important step.

When we follow the Holy Spirit, He will help us do whatever it takes to spread the gospel, no matter what color the light flashes beyond us.

God's No and God's Go

Every follower of Christ needs three different relationships.
1. A Paul to mentor and inspire faith.
2. A Barnabas to encourage along the way.
3. A Timothy to build up and assist in doing the work of the kingdom.

I've had all three in my life, and they've made me who I am today. We all need these relationships because ministry is more *caught* than *taught*. As we grow in our faith, we take on the spiritual habits and qualities of those around us consistently.

As Paul and Timothy move together to find where to take the gospel next, the Holy Spirit urges them to avoid Asia. The very thing you'd think the Spirit would urge them *to do,* He urges them *not* to do. In obedience they leave Asia and head to Europe. It is in Troas that the gospel spreads all over the world. This is such a pivotal moment in Paul's journey. After traveling north, south, east, and west, it's in Troas that the gospel launches. Here, Paul learned that God's *no* is just as important as God's *go*.

As the psalmist writes, "The steps of a man are established by the Lord, when he delights in his way; though he fall, he shall not

Day 17: Stops And Steps

be cast headlong, for the Lord upholds his hand" (Psalm 37:23-24). Isn't God's leading awesome? Not only are a man's *steps* established by the Lord, but also his stops. God will use the green, yellow, and red lights to bring his plans to pass. Each color is directed by Him.

At another event in Georgia, I served as an evangelist at a small Christian university with a talented girls softball team. I was asked to speak in the Chapel service on Monday but realized that many of the athletes were not in attendance. Later, I found out that most of the athletes at this college would skip the chapel service because they were too tired to get up from partying the night before. For the next two days, I decided to stay on campus and immerse myself in their environment. I went to the ball field and led a Bible study, visited the dorms, and had several conversations throughout the campus. Almost all my time was spent with the athletes, especially on the girls' softball team. By Wednesday night, over twenty softball players got saved and gave their lives to Christ!

Eagerly, they all wanted to get baptized, so I worked something out to make it happen. Everyone pulled their cars up to the local pool and shined their headlights on the cold water. It wasn't the most ideal setup, but it worked. One after the other dipped into the pool and committed their lives to Jesus. Some even got saved as they were watching their teammates get baptized and ended up jumping in the water to join them. It was truly an incredible night, and I knew God led me to this moment at the local pool.

Well, the next day, I got an email from the person who asked me to speak. She praised the way I ministered to the college students but added how I will probably never get asked back. When I asked why, she said the Baptist professors claimed it was blasphemous to baptize the students without the authority of the church behind it.

That conversation was disappointing to say the least. It was just another example of how getting caught up in the small, legalistic traditions can prevent the gospel from spreading. But as I pondered how God had been leading throughout that week, it was clear He was saying *Go*. Minister to these kids. Spend time with them. Love them. And that's exactly what I did.

We can't always prevent the red lights that are scattered on our journeys for Christ. But we can trust that God's hand is in every *no* just as it is in every *go*. I will never let a pesky *no* get in the way of sharing the way to salvation. Because when God is leading our steps (and our stops), we're sure to be successful along the way.

Wows and Woahs

Day 18

wow (exclamation): "to express astonishment or admiration"
woah (exclamation): "to express surprise or alarm (spiritual concern)"

"So he reasoned in the synagogue with the Jews and the devout persons…"

Acts 17:17

I recently read a statistic about the Christian population that, sadly, did not stun me: if current trends continue, Christians could make up less than half of the population in the United States by 2070.[5] In fact, the Christian population is trending to make up as little as one-third of the population in less than fifty years.

---

[5] Bob Smietana, "Fewer Than Half of Americans May Be Christian By 2070, According to New Projections," The Roys Report, September 13, 2022, https://julieroys.com/fewer-than-half-american-may-be-christian-by-2070-projections/.

It might even take less time than that. The state of the church today is in terrible shape; she is dwindling quickly, and what does remain is a shallow shell of what she should be.

However, there is hope. I want to remind you of the reason you started this modern-day journey into the ancient church in the first place. We decided to take this time to rediscover what was lost in order to help others discover the gospel. And we're doing this by looking back at old biblical principles that have never lost their power or relevancy. I believe we can change that scary statistic with God's hand and our commitment to looking backward.

At this point in our journey in the study of Acts, we see how Paul spread the message of the gospel from place to place, practically lighting each city on fire with his controversial message. We've seen how some people reject the gospel in an uproar and others willingly accept the message with boldness—something we still see in modern church mission trips.

But one thing's for sure: The same message that was spread during the ancient church through Paul's missionary journeys is the same message for our church today.

The gospel is enough. And it's for *everyone*.

But as we know, the gospel often brings opposition and persecution. In chapter 17, we read about Paul and Silas traveling to Thessalonica, where they were later sent out of the city due to certain unpersuaded Jews who gathered a mob of people and set the city in an uproar. After that, they were sent to Berea, where the same Jews followed them to stop the gospel message from spreading. This time, Silas and Timothy remain in Berea to plant a church and Paul went to Athens to continue spreading the message.

Don't you find it interesting that people are always gathering in crowds to fight against one man preaching about Jesus? And

Day 18: Wows And Woahs

yet, every time *the gospel still grows!* Throughout history, we see that the church often grows during times of persecution.

Paul wasn't afraid of the inevitable persecution in his call for the Lord. Instead, he pressed on in spreading the gospel, intuitively reading the crowds and culture of each city to learn best how to persuade them.

While his methods of persuasion may have changed from city to city, the message *never* did. He was confident that the message of the gospel was enough for *all* people. As we dive into the various ways Paul was able to persuade the crowd, I challenge you to reflect on the ways we might use his methods to expand our modern-day church so that by 2070, there will be more people who have accepted God's redeeming message of the gospel.

Reasoning the Gospel

Throughout the years, I've attended various Bible studies with people of different perspectives. In one particular Bible study group, a man made a comment that confused me. I wanted him to elaborate on what he meant and why he thought his comment to be true. He just muttered, "Because I said so."

No reasoning to explain his side. No explanation of what he meant. Just *because I said so*. While parents and teachers may use this as a quick escape from a longer conversation with a child, this statement hardly settles a curious adult's mind. And it wouldn't have settled the minds of the people in Thessalonica either.

Paul knew that "because I said so" would not be enough to persuade the people about the message of Jesus. That's why we read that he "reasoned with them from the Scriptures, explaining and proving that it was necessary for Christ to suffer and rise from the dead" (Acts 17:2-3). You see, *reasoning* means you are using logic or good sense in your dialogue on a topic. And Paul had a fantastic way of reasoning with every heart. Paul worked hard to understand the culture. He was kind and reasonable to the people in any given city. He would take the time to open up the truth to people and explain to them with detailed description. Finally, he would *demonstrate* the gospel. This means Paul would prove Jesus' resurrection by presenting evidence to convince the people. When you explain and prove something, you are demonstrating it.

Paul was always preaching in the way the people needed to receive the gospel. He wrote to the Corinthians, "I have become all things to all people, that by all means I might save some. I do it all for the sake of the gospel, that I may share with them in its blessings" (1 Corinthians 9 22-23).

Truly, he won *some*. Because three weeks after his conversation with the Thessalonians, a church was planted. Paul didn't need to gather a demographic study on the area because the gospel is for all people. There was no need for a rock star worship leader or amazing communicator because the Holy Spirit is what truly directs worship from the heart. No need to find a building because where two or more are gathered Jesus says He is there. No, Paul simply used the message of the gospel to win the people of Thessalonica. It's a message for *all* people, and it's enough for *everyone*.

It was enough then, and it's still enough today. In our modern day, it can be tempting to think you need all of those worldly resources in a box to draw people in the doors. But the truth is you don't need any of that to persuade others for the gospel.

After some time, however, the Jews who were not persuaded by Paul's preaching gathered angry crowds in an uproar. Paul had officially worn out his welcome and was sent to Berea with Silas. His use of reasoning and logic would continue to win people for the gospel, just in different cities and environments. Paul would soon enter two new cities, spreading the gospel and finding new ways to reason with the crowds—even with crowds that seem the least likely to ever say yes to Jesus.

If Paul Went to Vegas

Have you ever been to Sin City?

It's quite the place. More times than not, it lives up to its nickname.

People come from far and wide to sightsee and tour Vegas. One of the first things many people think when they see the glitter of the city is *Wow!* As the definition of the word says, they view the city with astonishment and admiration.

Wow! The lights are captivating.

Wow! The shows are fabulous.

Wow! The city is a complete party.

However, my first reaction to Sin City was less like *"wow"* and more like *"woah."* I was there for a motivational speaking event that I was asked to do. For accountability, I always take one of my three boys with me on a trip. This time, I went with my son Jeremiah.

As we walked the streets, I couldn't help but be alarmed by the darkness of sin that lingered on every corner.

Woah. There's an intense indulgence in booze, drugs, and gambling.

Woah. There are prostitutes and vulgar shows advertised everywhere.

Woah. These people are far from God.

Even after speaking at the morning session, this heaviness lingered inside of me.

The Revenant

I bet Paul must have felt a similar feeling when he entered Athens after being sent out of Thessalonica and then Berea. You see, when Paul and Silas entered Berea after leaving the uproar in Thessalonica, they went straight to the Jewish synagogue. But the opposition kept following Paul in the wake of his missions. And those unpersuaded Jews who were in an uproar in Thessalonica made their way to Berea when they heard of Paul's continued preaching. With that, Paul left for Athens.

Upon entering Athens, Paul's spirit was provoked by the heaviness of sin. Athens was a city full of idols and religion. The people there were well educated and well cultured, but they had not received the message of the gospel. I can't help but wonder if Paul's initial reaction was much like mine when I walked the streets of Vegas.

Woah. These people have thirty thousand gods.

Woah. They believe that humanity started randomly by some particles joining together.

Woah. This city is full of sinners.

"I really feel like I need to get outta here," I told my wife over the phone after a heavy night in Vegas with Jeremiah. "This is my last trip to this city. The darkness of sin is too much. I really don't think I'll be coming back."

"But Christian," my wife said, "God loves those people too. They need the gospel too."

Her words rang true in my ears. But I still needed to get away from the city for a couple of hours, so I decided to take Jeremiah on a short road trip to see one of the Seven Wonders of the Industrial World, the Hoover Dam. It was only an hour away from Vegas, and being the former NASCAR Chaplin that I am, I rented a new 5.0 Mustang to create a fun memory with my son before my speaking session that night. We busted down the highway singing to the radio and enjoying the views.

Day 18: Wows And Woahs

As I drove, the secular song "Drive" by Incubus was playing on the station. They have a line that says, *Whatever tomorrow brings, I will be there.* The song goes on to sing about water and wine, obviously referencing Jesus' miracle. Just as I heard that lyric, we were going under an overpass where we passed an eighteen-wheeler going the opposite direction, heading into Vegas. On the side of the truck were the words "Jesus Christ is Lord." For me, it was almost as if God were saying, "As you are *leaving* the city because of the sin, someone else is *entering* the city because of the sin."

Maybe that truck driver would drive up to the lights of Vegas and *not* say, "Wow!"

Maybe he'd say, *"Woah."*

Woah. The city has the potential for salvation.

Woah. God could do something for the people here.

Woah. I have to do something about it.

See, when Paul saw Athens for the first time, he didn't see it as a sightseer *or* an onlooker of sin. When Paul saw Athens, he didn't think, *"Wow"* but *"Woah."*

Woah. I have to do something about what I see.

Woah. I have to tell these people about Jesus.

Woah. God could do amazing things in this city.

Paul did not change his message of the gospel to better fit the Epicurean beliefs of the city. Rather, he civilly confronted the religious culture. (After all, a Roman satirist once described ancient Athens by saying that it's easier to find a god there than a man.)

By God's perfect leading, Paul noticed one of the thirty thousand statues in Athens that read The Unknown God. Just in case, the Athenians had a statue of a god they may have forgotten. What a miracle that Paul saw that statue out of all thirty thousand of them because he used it to reason with the Athenians. Paul let them know that he knows who the unknown god is—the one who loves them and died on the cross for their sins.

We can all follow Paul's lead when it comes to reasoning with the people in our own circles about the gospel. It doesn't require words that wow the crowd or songs that awe the listeners. It simply requires the profound message of the gospel and a heart that looks at a broken city and dares to say, *"Woah."*

Prep Rallies

Day 19

"Let every action of mine be something beautiful for God."
Saint Teresa of Calcutta

"And the Lord said to Paul one night in a vision, 'Do not be afraid, but go on speaking and do not be silent, for I am with you, and no one will attack you to harm you, for I have many in this city who are my people.' And he stayed a year and six months, teaching the word of God among them."

Acts 18:9-11

If you could have one person in the world—alive or dead—pray over you, who would it be? Perhaps you would choose a mighty disciple like Paul or John. Maybe the one that sparked the fire that started the great Reformation, Martin Luther. Or even a great Christian author or man of faith like C. S. Lewis.

My answer to that question starts at the Billy Graham Library in Charlotte, North Carolina. Before leaving town to speak at an evangelical outreach event, I'd always go to the Billy Graham

Library. This place is a forty-thousand-square-foot experience of the life of the American evangelist. I'd walk through the tour that presented the journey of his life through multimedia presentations, photos, and stories. Each new space of time revealed something extraordinary and inspiring from his past—something that would give me new insight and inspiration into this evangelical work.

Walking through each room and gallery, I'd then venture outside to where Billy and his wife are laid to rest. Toward the end of my time, I'd sit on the bench outside and listen to hymns, reflecting quietly on the trip ahead. As I'd walk back through the library on my way out, I'd never leave without visiting a certain elderly gentleman relaxing in a rocking chair. Every time I visited, the same man would be sitting in that chair, moving back and forth as he admired the scenery.

He was such a valued guest to the library that his name—Reverend Fleet Kirkpatrick—was put on that rocking chair. Reverend Fleet was a pastor of over fifty years in Charlotte at a small, traditional church of about fifty people. Whenever I'd approach him in that rocking chair, I'd ask him to pray for me. And without a doubt, he'd reach over and grab my hand. His spotted and worn hands were as comforting as his gentle spirit. As he rocked back and forth in that chair, he prayed that God would keep me safe and pour his blessings down upon me.

This small-time pastor was probably never asked to speak at a large ministry conference. He probably never preached from a big stage or arena. I'm not sure that many people in the faith community even knew of him. But me? I attribute much of my success to this man. If I had a choice of anyone in the world to pray over me, alive or dead, I would choose Reverend Fleet. Though his education or credentials were not impressive, his passion to serve and live life for the kingdom was. Reverend

Day 19: Prep Rallies

Fleet was the definition of what it means to be faithful. He's the kind of person I aspire to be.

What about you? If I had to guess, I bet the person you chose has similar qualities. Someone with bold faith, courageous spirit, passionate heart, and faithful steadfastness for the Lord.

In chapter 18 of the book of Acts, we get a real glimpse of what it means to have a true transformational change like those we admire as our personal prayer warriors. As Reverend Fleet showed with his life, Paul also showed in the evangelistic work throughout the city of Corinth. Let's unpack the qualities of evangelism we can learn from Paul in chapter 18.

The Ability to Connect

Paul was ministering to people in the city of Corinth. This place was filled with buildings famous for its Corinthian bronze pillars. It was also known for sports, second only to those held in Olympia. Corinth was also known for its infamous debauchery. So much so that when anyone acted badly around that region, they were said to have acted like a Corinthian.

Just outside the city stood the Temple of Aphrodite, the goddess of love. Though it was in ruins by the time Paul visited, still a thousand prostitutes stayed by this temple to do their work. Sailors and traveling salesmen would gladly spend time with the prostitutes, which is why the city was known for its immorality.

This was the city Paul was preaching to. And while he was facing the amazing architecture, he was also facing the greatest depths of sin and evil. In this dark and sinful environment, Paul knew he had to connect to the culture. He needed to do so in order to gain the credibility and respect to be heard by the city. So he got to know the culture. In Corinth all the fathers taught their

The Revenant

children a trade. One Jewish saying went like this: "If you don't teach your son a trade, you teach your son to steal." The Jewish fathers placed a high value on working a trade, so that's exactly what Paul did.

Paul became a tentmaker so that he could connect with the culture of Corinth and use his job as a place to preach about Jesus. What better example can we modern-day Christians find to connect to? The culture of America is like Corinth, full of sin, evil, and selfish desires. In our jobs, we have an opportunity to preach the gospel just like Paul did. Yes, Paul's tentmaking put food on the table, and your job does too. But what's more, your job can be a way to bring people into an eternal relationship with Jesus Christ. It all starts with connecting with the culture.

One of my first speaking opportunities was a huge Salvation Army event in Birmingham, Alabama, with thousands of predominantly African American students. The MC of the event, knowing my bio, introduced me as the winner of *Reality Racing: The Rookie Challenge,* a reality TV show on Spike TV where I was regarded as the NASCAR Chaplain and picked up the nickname the Faster Pastor. He added that I was from Kannapolis, North Carolina, home of Dale Earnheart, and raced in the Baja 1000, the most dangerous race in Baja, Mexico.

After this grand introduction literally nobody clapped. And as I walked onstage and passed the host, I joked, "Could you have made me sound any whiter?"

It took at least fifteen minutes to break through to the audience after that introduction. After that I vowed to get to know the culture of the communities where I was to speak.

Not long after the Birmingham event, I traveled to Charlotte to speak to a similar audience. This time, I decided to start differently. During my time as a youth pastor, I found that I had a creative gift for rapping. I would take secular rap songs like

Dr. Dre and Snoop Dogg's "Nothing But a G Thang" and put Christian lyrics over them. These songs would loosen up the crowd and allow them to connect to what I was saying.

As silly as it sounds, there is always a cultural connection you have to learn before ministering to people. The only way to do that is to do what Paul did—you must assimilate yourself into the culture. Spend days in the community. Speak to the people. Visit places in the area. Attend services. Get to know the families. Because the truth is that the gospel will always be life-changing, but people's hearts have to be opened to receive it.

Paul did the work of connecting because he knew how important it was to build a foundation with people. He wrote, "For though I am free from all, I have made myself a servant to all, that I might win more of them" (1 Corinthians 9:19), and he truly lived that way.

In Thessalonica, the people had a fondness for Old Testament Scriptures, so he preached that Jesus was the fulfillment of Old Testament Scriptures. In Athens, the slogan was "man is great," because their teaching was built on the belief system of man's greatness. So Paul used those beliefs and preached man is *not* great, but God is. Wherever he went, he had a way to connect people to the gospel. The ability to connect will be the first quality to learn from Paul so that we can help bring others to Christ.

Prep Rallies, Not Pep Rallies

When I was in high school and played football, all the students, players, and cheerleaders would gather in the gym for a pep rally. The purpose of these cheesy gatherings was to celebrate the team, pump up the students, and calm the athletes' nerves

The Revenant

before the big game—where we were crushed most of the time. So what good was the pep rally?

If you think about it, many churches today are there for a pep rally, when they should really be there for a *prep* rally. As we enter the new week as Christians ready to evangelize to our community like Paul, it can be a nerve-racking feeling. *How will they react? What will I say? Will they judge me or respond to my words?*

That's why at church, we need less of a pep rally and more of a *prep* rally to get us ready to evangelize. Did you know that the phrase "Do not be afraid" appears in the Bible 365 times? One for every single day of the year. God knew it was *that* important and *that* needed! Without a doubt, it can be scary to talk to others about the gospel. Paul was working diligently in the city of Corinth, trying to culturally connect people with the gospel, but he was hitting a ton of roadblocks. Each place he stopped, Paul became wearier and wearier. After all, when you're known as a Corinthian, you're known as a bad person. Paul was afraid he would not be able to be successful in his mission for the Lord, but God said otherwise. The Lord spoke to Paul in a vision and told him not to be afraid or be silent, for He was with him. So that's exactly what Paul kept on doing.

Three Promises for Living a Transformational Life

Paul was living a full-out transformational life in Corinth and encouraging others to do so as well. When we Christians are living this transformational life through the Holy Spirit, God gives us three promises.

First, God promises He is with us. He promises the ministry of His presence.

Second, God promises He will protect us, just like He promised Paul in Corinth.

Third, God promises that He has plans for us, so we need not worry about the roadblocks along the way.

By living a transformational life that can sometimes be scary, these promises are ones we can cling to no matter what. We can trust that God will lead us place after place, and will close the door when it's time to leave. We don't need a pep rally. We need a *prep* rally to be fully equipped with the tools we need to evangelize. We need to be taught the promises of God so that we can boldly share the gospel when the Holy Spirit prompts. As we follow the example of Paul, we can connect the Word of God to each environment boldly to impact the culture to the greatest extent.

Passion and Action

When I was searching for a job before coming to New Life, I noticed that most of the openings required a seminary degree. Education seems to be of the utmost importance in ministering, but is that really what's most important?

There are two greater qualities above education when it comes to being an effective minister, evangelist, or Christ follower: passion and action.

When our passion for the kingdom of God overflows from our hearts, it is demonstrated in transformational actions. And actions? That's how a true impact can be made in people's lives.

Take a recent story from Albuquerque, New Mexico. This area has a long history of European ideas about witches and blends with traditions from Mexican, Spanish, and Native cultures. A church was planted in the area and was just starting to grow in the community. When a group of local witches got together and heard about this church, they started working to stop the church from growing. Some of them even threatened to burn the church down if they wouldn't stop sharing the gospel.

The pastor just laughed. "The building is metal. How are you going to burn it?"

After a few more minutes of comical banter, one of the witches, who was also a self-proclaimed Satanist, agreed to meet with the pastor because of his sense of humor. At the meeting, somehow, some way this pastor was able to connect with the Satanist. He ended up giving his life to Christ at that very meeting and apologized to the people he scared with his threats. Because of the actions of the pastor to love those who were different from him, a transformation occurred in the least likely of hearts.

Action can go a long way. But if we take a good look at the facts, we're not the best at acting. Statistics show that globally, people average 6 hours and 58 minutes of screen time a day.[6] That is almost a full-time job being useless or unproductive scrolling on TikTok or binging Netflix. Many Christians have found other hobbies that get in the way of transformational living. But like Paul, if we want to make a true change in our communities, we must use our passion to prioritize action.

He was never about a pep rally. Paul knew above all that the Holy Spirit inside of him is what was truly great. The way he lived his life with people was all about *prepping* them for what was to come—and if you know anything about history, you know the nightmare that was soon to come under the rule of Nero. (After all, what good is a pep rally when your family is about to be put on a stake and set on fire for the gospel by the new emperor?)

In our communities and faith circles, may we follow Paul's lead. Let our passion and action transform our churches into a prep rally for the ages.

---

[6] Simon Kemp, "Digital 2022: Global Overview Report," *Data Reportal,* January 26, 2022, https://datareportal.com/reports/digital-2022-global-overview-report.

Who Knows Your Name?

Day 20

"Give a man an electric shock, and I warrant you he will know it; but if he has the Holy Ghost, he will know it much more."
Charles Spurgeon

"But the evil spirit answered them, 'Jesus I know, and Paul I recognize, but who are you?'"

Acts 19:15

At this point in Paul's missions, plenty of people began to know the name of Jesus. And many began to remember the name of Paul too.

Paul, the people person.

Paul, the apostle.

Paul, the saint.

Oh, and Paul, the destroyer of our culture, community, and economy.

The Revenant

It's safe to say that those who opposed Paul and the message he spread were incredibly unhappy with the havoc he was wreaking in their cities, Ephesus being one of them.

This city was known as a stronghold of Satan. The people there were deeply influenced by satanic rituals and superstitious practices. In fact, one of the biggest economic influences in Ephesus was a temple that many would frequent for fertility and marital blessings—the temple of Diana, also known as Artemis.

Diana was the goddess of the hunt and the protector of young girls. The sixty-foot-high temple was regarded as one of the seven wonders of the ancient world. The (quite frankly, frightening-looking) statue of Diana is a multi-breasted figure with a face and a grain measure on her head. When a couple planned to get married, they would cut off the bride's hair and place it in the temple as a sacrifice to bless their marriage.

You can imagine what the message of the gospel did to this pagan city when the Holy Spirit came upon them. Satanic and spiritual books were burned, people stopped visiting the temple of Diana, and visitors quit buying superstitious items from Ephesus. All of these reactions to Paul's message changed Ephesus' culture, community, and economy.

While the name of Jesus was praised on the new believers' lips, the name of Paul was cursed under the pagan city's breath. You see, both groups of people knew Paul's name well because of his persistent work for Jesus.

Throughout this chapter, the question I challenge you to keep at the forefront of your mind is this: Who knows your name?

When the Holy Spirit Comes Upon You

As Paul entered Ephesus, he came across some disciples and asked them if they had received the Holy Spirit when they were

Day 20: Who Knows Your Name?

baptized. Confused, they answered, "No, we haven't even heard that there is a Holy Spirit. . . [We were baptized] into John's baptism" (Acts 19:2-3).

These believers were, in fact, *not* believers. They did not realize they were separated from God because of their sin or that Jesus was raised from the dead and gave the Holy Spirit to produce a real understanding in their hearts. Just because they'd heard of John's baptism didn't mean they were saved. These disciples missed the biggest part—Jesus. Paul went on to tell them about Jesus and laid hands on them. In turn, they received the Holy Spirit. *Now,* they were saved!

In my own pastoring, I have come across thousands of people who claim to be a believer and when I ask why they believe they are saved, they can't explain it. They can't give a clear-cut explanation as to why they are a believer. Some say, "I believe in God because I know he loves me" or "I believe God created everything, so I am a Christian." There are many politicians and pastors who resist standing up for the name of Jesus but will stand for the name of God. But just as Paul wanted the disciples in Ephesus to understand, *it's so much deeper than that.*

Salvation does not come from knowing Bible stories or going to church as a kid.

It's deeper than following your boyfriend or girlfriend to an altar call.

It's certainly beyond wearing a WWJD bracelet or sticking a fish on your car window.

The truth is that the Holy Spirit has to enter you in order for you to live a life for the gospel. Acts 1:8 says that you will receive power when the Holy Spirit comes upon you. Without the Holy Spirit, you only have potential not power. This is where true transformational change happens. See, Christian baptism

The Revenant

doesn't look at what *you* do but at what *Christ* has done. And when you are baptized in the Spirit, you are empowered to live a life worthy of his calling.

But change means actions. There are a lot of people today in church that just go along with Jesus without ever truly understanding or receiving the Spirit. To them, Jesus says, "I never knew you; depart from me, you workers of lawlessness" (Matthew 7:23). That's why it's important to consider if someone were to look at your life, would they notice the power of the Holy Spirit? Or would they notice His absence? When you get to heaven's gates, will your name be recognized?

Of course, the Lord knows the name of every single one of His children because they are His divine creation. But it's up to us to decide to embrace the love of Christ and develop a relationship with Him or to walk away from Him forever. Revelation 3:5 says, "the one who conquers will be clothed thus in white garments, and I will never blot his name out of the book of life. I will confess his name before my Father and before his angels." Will your name be known?

I ask you to reflect on this quote from famous preacher Charles Spurgeon: "Have ye then received the Spirit since you believed? Beloved, are you now receiving the Spirit? Are you living under his divine influence? Are you filled with his power? Put the question personally. I am afraid some professors will have to admit that they hardly know whether there be any Holy Ghost; and others will have to confess that though they have enjoyed a little of his saving work, yet they do not know much of his ennobling and sanctifying influence."[7]

---

[7] Charles Haddon Spurgeon, "Receiving the Holy Ghost," Sermon at Metropolitan Tabernacle Pulpit Volume 30, July 13, 1884, https://www.spurgeon.org/resource-library/sermons/receiving-the-holy-ghost/#flipbook/.

Day 20: Who Knows Your Name?

Paul noticed the lack of power and righteousness in the disciples throughout Ephesus, and he made it a personal mission to ensure they received the Holy Spirit. In turn, many more people made their name known to Christ and would one day enter the kingdom of heaven.

The same can be true for us. We must only make our name known through the transformational power of the Holy Spirit.

Persistence Over Complacency

As Paul continued to stir things up in Ephesus through this great revival, he sent Timothy and Erastus to Macedonia while he stayed in the city. And through every single hint of opposition, Paul persisted in his mission for Jesus and began working miracles through his hands.

God would heal people through Paul's sweaty handkerchiefs and aprons without him even being present. This was quite unusual, but it goes to show that God was willing to work through any means to draw the people of Ephesus closer to Him. After seeing all of Paul's miracles, however, some of the Jewish exorcists decided to copy what they believed Paul was doing through superstition. They said to the sick people, We "adjure you by the Jesus whom Paul proclaims. . . But the evil spirit answered them, 'Jesus I know, and Paul I know; but who are you?' " (Acts 19:13, 15). After that, the evil spirits leaped on them, wounded them, and stripped them naked.

That brings us back to the original question: Who knows your name? Better yet, Is your name known in hell?

Even the demons in hell knew the name of Paul. That's because the demons in hell know the names of its enemies. The men who attempted to heal the people without the power of the Holy Spirit were unknown to the demons. And they weren't known to Jesus either. Grasped onto the coattails of Paul's faith would never be enough for salvation.

But Paul was so persistent in his passion for the gospel that the very demons in hell shook in their boots. His name was not just known, it was feared. Although he was put on trial, persecuted, and imprisoned, Paul never stopped his mission for the gospel.

He was a true visionary. Through Paul's example, we learn that one presentation of the gospel should always lead to another opportunity. Not too long ago, I was asked to speak at a public school where there was a Fellowship of Christian Athletes (FCA) event before the school day began. There were about one hundred kids, but my focus was preaching the gospel to FCA students and serving the staff while I was there. As I entered the front office of the middle school on my way to speak at the FCA event there was a student who was being confronted because he wasn't caught up on his breakfast bill. The Lord prompted me to do something to help this student. As I rested in the Spirit, I remembered how persistent Paul was about serving others and encouraging them with the hope of the gospel. Why just help one student if I can help all of them? So I asked the assistant principal to gather all the students in the school who were behind on payments. "That's an interesting question," she responded, "Why?"

"Our church wants to help all the students who are behind on payments to get caught up. We'd also like to pay for them for the rest of the year," I replied.

You see, it would have been reasonable and easy for me to say, "I just spoke to a hundred kids in FCA. That's enough." But like Paul, you must think out of the box. An opportunity to speak at FCA to share the gospel led to another opportunity to help pay for the students' breakfast, and then another opportunity to cater lunch for all the teachers at the school. That's what it

Day 20: Who Knows Your Name?

means to be a visionary. If we're too closed off to see it, we'll remain complacent.

When we become complacent in our walk with Christ, we quit spending time in His Word daily. When we become complacent in our jobs, we stay in the same place forever because of the salary. When we become complacent in our relationships, we never get the courage to tell our unbelieving friends about Christ. Complacency is the enemy of progress.

As I continue to rebuild this traditional church here in South Carolina, I've been seeking guidance and wisdom from pastors in the area. There is a megachurch nearby that seems to be very successful with its incredible kids' ministry, college ministry, and large attendance every Sunday. I decided to contact the pastor for a quick meeting to ask him a question about the community I had been called to reach because I knew he had years of experience in building a successful church in the local community. I also wanted to ask him to pray for me about some concerns I had about the church I was pastoring. I called and left a message for him, only to receive a callback from his secretary telling me he did not have time to meet with me or even speak on the phone, because he was in the middle of building his new home. Though I understand that we all have lives to live outside the four walls of the church, I can't imagine a time where anyone serving in the book of Acts would turn down an opportunity to love people and share the gospel.

When we get beyond the comfort of complacency, we begin to make ripples of change in the lives of those around us. Paul took on the beast of Ephesus, one of the most pagan cities in the world. The riot was huge, but his persistence held strong. Because of that, many were saved by the power of the Holy Spirit.

So, as we close today's reading, I ask for the final time: Who knows your name?

The Revenant

You don't have to be known in cities or countries around the world, and you don't have to be the most popular person at your school or job. But by living your daily life sensitive to the gentle prompting of the Holy Spirit, your name will certainly be known.

Lights, Camera, ~~Action~~ Tears!

⑂AY 21

"It's never goodbye. It's 'until we meet again.'"
Unknown

"But I do not account my life of any value nor as precious to myself, if only I may finish my course and the ministry that I received from the Lord Jesus, to testify to the gospel of the grace of God."

Acts 20:24

Can you recall the most epic scene in your favorite movie?

How about the ending scene in *Braveheart*? The one where William Wallace tells Queen Isabella, *"Every man dies, not every man really lives."* Or the scene from *The Notebook*, where the elderly couple hold hands and die together? And you can't forget the moment in *Saving Private Ryan* when Captain John H. Miller lays down his life so Private Ryan can get back safely to his family.

The Revenant

Many epic Hollywood films like these oftentimes contain great love stories that become the key to the entire movie. And as the credits roll when the movie comes to an end, you're left with some tears in your eyes and a changed heart.

Why? Because in those scenes, you're reminded of the reason the story was told in the first place.

Whatever movie you think of when you envision an epic moment, this chapter of Acts is that Hollywood scene. The credits rolled on Paul's fruitful two years in Ephesus, and the impact he had on the disciples lingered in the forefront of their minds. Tears from Paul's eyes began to wet the sand as he gave his final regards to the people, knowing he would never see them again.

Like watching the epic moments in movies, I can imagine it was difficult to live through this moment in Ephesus. It's as if it was said before the scene started, "Lights, camera, *tears!*" And everyone started to cry.

Sometimes, it's hard to accept moments like this in our faith journeys. Saying goodbye to mentors. Moving away from your home church. Watching students in your youth group graduate. Being rejected after sharing the gospel.

Realistically, though, the tears that fall in our own stories are actually a huge part of having viable faith. It probably took Paul everything in him to continue his journey away from Ephesus, but he knew it was time to go. And it was good for him to mourn the end of a scene in his story. Most important, he didn't let the scene end without encouraging the people to be a successful church.

So without further ado, let's dive into Paul's final scene in Ephesus to reflect on the most important lessons he taught through the Holy Spirit during his time there.

Lights, camera, ~~action!~~ *tears!*

Day 21: Lights, Camera, Action Tears!

Be Productive While You're Here

Before saying his final goodbye to the Ephesians, Paul made a trip to Greece and Macedonia. He didn't simply pop in for a day and say, "Hey guys, how are you doing? Have a great day!" No, Paul stayed for three months. He ate with them, lived among them, and encouraged them. Winter was a bad time to travel on the Mediterranean Sea, so Paul decided to use his time wisely.

Some people claim Paul was "stuck," and that might be so. Stuck or not Paul knew he was going to be productive with the time God had given him. Whatever the season, he would preach the gospel, making the most of every opportunity to witness to the people.

A major part of productivity is remembering that the season you're in is not always about you. Some seasons of life come through with a gust of wind and other times they come in with a hailstorm. Whatever the season, Paul reminds us about the importance of making the most of the time God gives you through his productivity in Greece. He hunkered down in this season for three months, and do you know what happened to the people he ministered to?

Well, we don't know. All of those men were never heard from again. Yet they helped Paul accomplish his ministry. God will use every moment He gives you for the betterment of His Kingdom.

Paul chose to spend hours upon hours during his time in each city preaching God's Word to the people. At this time, before Constantine, the pagans worshiped the god of the sun on Sundays and the god of Saturn on Saturdays. But to Paul, every day was a day of worship. He knew that he would probably never see these people again, so he had to make much of the time he had with them. After all, when you're busy with the Lord, you never know who you'll minister to. Every now and then, Paul would encounter a famous person while preaching. Homer the poet and Pythagoras the mathematician were two examples, and Paul never changed his message. He taught the truth of the gospel day after day.

And when Paul taught, *Paul taught*.

He didn't believe in sermonettes that produced Christianettes! In fact, the day before Paul was going to leave Troas, he decided to preach until midnight to be as productive as possible. Well, a young man named Eutychus (whose name means "fortunate") fell asleep during this long sermon. In his daze, he fell out of the third-story window, crashing to the ground. Luke, the doctor, was there with Paul when this happened, and he said the boy was dead. Taking cues from Elijah, Paul resurrected Eutychus through God's power.

Perhaps God taught the people through Eutychus that our boredom and complacency in the church need to be resurrected for us to be productive. A modern-day pastor once said that he knows people sleep during his sermon for multiple reasons. Maybe they worked late, maybe they have a sleeping disorder, maybe they're on medication—or maybe he's simply boring. But you know what? He was okay with all of those reasons because at least they were in church. He'd rather have someone catch a message while sleeping than miss all of it with a sleeping heart.

That's why Paul tells the Roman church that it's time for them to wake up from their sleep (Romans 13:11). And it's why he makes the most of every moment he has, even when it meant resurrecting a sleeping young man.

While we're here, we must be productive in the name of the Lord. You simply never know the monumental scene in someone's life that God will impact all because you chose to be productive.

Day 21: Lights, Camera, Action Tears!

The Final Goodbye

If Paul's journey was truly a movie, the moment he sent for the elders of Ephesus would be the beginning of the movie's epic, unforgettable scene. The scene that the entire movie was built around.

As he began to say goodbye to the Ephesians forever, he said that from the first day he came to them, he served the Lord with humility (Acts 20:18-19). When I first read this, I was reminded of the moment Paul spoke to the Corinthians when he said, "For now we see in a mirror dimly, but then face to face. Now I know in part; then I shall know fully, even as I have been fully known" (1 Corinthians 13:12).

It's important to note that back then, they didn't have mirrors. The only way they saw their reflection was through polished steel, which is not very helpful when trying to see yourself. Polished steel doesn't give a clear reflection. But the point that Paul was making was that he wasn't supposed to see himself clearly but see *others* more clearly. Paul didn't give account to his own life in his goodbyes to the Ephesians but gave value to others over himself.

One of my neighbors is a builder. I have intentionally spent time loving on him and showing him the gospel. The other day, I received a letter from my HOA saying that my pine needles looked bad. So I decided to take a note from Paul and pine needle my house and both my neighbors' houses. I ended up spending over $200 and spent all day on my hands and knees, laying pine straw at both the houses.

I wanted them to be encouraged. I wanted them to say, "Wow! He's a pastor and loves God." After I did that, I called my neighbor and asked if he would want to try coming to my church.

"You gotta start the new year off right, man!" I encouraged him.

The Revenant

"Well, we'd love to go, but my wife and our kids love this other church around the corner," he replied, referring to the megachurch in the area. Interestingly enough, it was the same church where the pastor was too busy building his new home to meet with me. I have to be honest; I was livid! How could he be going to the megachurch when I just pine-needled his entire yard?!

But that's when the Spirit of God said to me, "I had you pine needle the house to get them to go *to* church, not *a church*. At the end of the day, they are hearing the gospel."

I felt the Lord humble me at that moment. And I believe that's the same goodbye message Paul was giving to the church at Ephesus. It's true that we live in a world where many evangelists live highly and think highly. But Paul? He never coveted silver, gold, or good apparel. He came with the humility of the Holy Spirit and believed the kingdom worked through him. He didn't boast about *what* he had but about *who* he had. By living a full life of integrity, Paul had no regrets. And to the church in Ephesus, he cried when he said goodbye, but *not* with regrets, only with the wisdom and love that he first carried into the city.

Paul left the city ready to encourage the elders with integrity and vision. He wanted to leave them with nothing but the tools for success in their church. And with that, I will give you a few characteristics I believe a church needs to be successful.

7 Characteristics of a Successful Church

The people of a successful church . . .
1. **Live openly like Paul.** The early church broke bread together, laughed together, mourned together, and did life together. I am completely convinced after thirty

Day 21: Lights, Camera, Action Tears!

years in ministry, the majority of people that give their life to Christ don't do it at a church service but rather in the journey of life as they interact and experience the love of Jesus extended to them through Christians who understand the importance of fulfilling the Great Commission.

D. L. Moody gave his life to Christ not at church but when his Sunday School teacher went to visit him at his father's shoe shop where he repaired and resoled shoes. Martin Luther gave his life to Christ when he was caught in the middle of a violent lightning storm and cried out to the heavens to be saved. John Wesley had a transformational kingdom experience when he was on a boat full of Moravion Christians who were unafraid by a turbulent sea that could sink their boat. In the midst of Wesley's fear of death, he realized he didn't have what they had and asked the Lord to fill his heart with Christ Jesus.

Paul encountered lost people and capitalized on those random relationships by sharing the gospel, and the church grew!

When we live out our daily lives through the Holy Spirit's leading, people are sure to notice something different in us. This is when we can share the gospel and help others give their lives to Christ.

2. **Are humble.** I'm reminded of a church planting pastor who didn't have enough volunteers early in his church plant, so he set up all the chairs and prayed over them before service on Saturday night himself. Soon the church grew and volunteers signed up to help. Though he gave them opportunities to serve in other areas, he decided in humility to keep serving the Lord by setting up and

praying over all the chairs on Saturday night. Soon he was able to hire a worship leader who was very gifted. When his first weekend came to serve the pastor asked him to help him set up chairs and pray over them on Saturday night. After hearing this the worship leader complained that he was not hired to stack chairs but lead worship. In response, the pastor said, "Well, I don't want to hold you back from greatness, so this is not going to work out." The pastor believed humility is the core foundation of every successful church.

3. **Will have hardships.** Historically, the church grows during hardships. If you're not having hardships, you're not showing characteristics of a New Testament church.

    After 9/11, churches all over America were filled to almost 90 percent capacity with hurt, lost, and angry souls reaching out for answers. But week by week, the numbers continued to shift down to where they were before. Today, church attendance is at an all-time low. In 2001, the church was not prepared to share the gospel.

    This is why we must not run from hardships but embrace them. By presenting a relational gospel rather than a religious gospel, we will be prepared for the revival that God brings our way. After all, He is the same yesterday, today, and will do the same for us in all our tomorrows if we faithfully endure the challenges that the Enemy brings our way.

4. **Have balance.** This balance is one between preaching and teaching. You must not only tell the sheep *what* to do but *how* to do it.

    Years ago, I heard a true story of a shepherd outside Jerusalem who owns a sheep farm and allows tourists to come and see the traditions of a biblical shepherd.

Day 21: Lights, Camera, Action Tears!

One group of tourists came but the sheep were nowhere to be seen, so they asked the shepherd where they were grazing. He told them they were on the other side of the mountain and, desiring to seize the opportunity, asked them to call the sheep to come so they could see them. One by one the tourists did their best to attract the sheep with different types of calls, and one by one they gave up. The shepherd then shouted over the hill just one time, and the entire herd came running. The tourists asked how that was possible, and the shepherd explained to them he spends time with the sheep. He cares for the sheep. He gives them medicine when they are sick and feeds them when they are hungry, so they recognize his voice and his voice alone. He then shared with them the word of Jesus: "My sheep hear my voice, and I know them, and they follow me" (John 10:27). A church should be led by an anointed shepherd who not only preaches and teaches but is willing to show the example of the gospel by doing life with the sheep and not hiding out in the green room or in his office five days a week. Not just about your talk but about your walk that brings about balance.

5. **Are sensitive to the Holy Spirit.** When Paul was suffering in jail, he wrote the book of Philippians. He was sensitive to the Holy Spirit's call to share what he was enduring, and the modern church must be too.

    I was raised in a Wesleyan Church, but have served in various denominations: Assembly of God, Lutheran, Methodist, Baptist, and nondenominational. As an itinerant speaker, I have spoken in every other denomination not mentioned! One thing I know to be true. No matter *what* the sign in front of your church says, if you're open and sensitive to the Holy Spirit, He will be in attendance and open the hearts of people.

And while I have seen some churches misuse the Holy Spirit's gifts, there must be balance and integrity when it comes to our time of gathering. Without a doubt, there is a fine line we must walk when it comes to this topic, but the Bible is clear on helping us walk that line with integrity.

If you're looking for a modern-day example of the power of a Spirit-filled church (outside the Word of God), I suggest reading *Fresh Wind, Fresh Fire* by Jim Cymbala. I read this book after graduating from college, and it changed my understanding of what it means to live a Spirit-filled life.

6. **Are determined.** It's important that the modern church steps boldly into the future with determination. R. W. Dale is an Alabama preacher that said the only preacher he knows to preach on hell with tears in his eyes is D. L. Moody. Similarly, when Paul talked about Jerusalem, there were tears in his eyes.

Early on in my ministry, I was shocked to find out how very few church members were interested in sharing the gospel with their communities. They went to work, to school, to the gym, to athletic practice, to the grocery store, and never seemed to want to share the gospel with the lost. I have to admit, from the rising of the sun to the setting of the same, I am *always* ready to share the gospel message of hope as Peter encourages us to do: "Be prepared to make a defense to anyone who asks you for a reason for the hope that is in you" (1 Peter 3:15). You never know when God will give you an opportunity to share His message, just like you'll never know the impact that it might have on the world.

7. **Teach the fullness of the gospel.** We are called to protect the message of the gospel. Psalm 23 famously says that thy rod and thy staff comfort me (v. 4, KJV). To guide the sheep, shepherds would gently use one end of the rod. The other side of the rod had nails and glass on the end to protect the sheep against wolves. As pastors, we are called to use both sides of the rod. We must gently guide our people, but also be ready to deal with the wolves.

The truth is that our western culture is overflowing with churches that are missing the mark on teaching about the fullness of the gospel. There are those that focus on grace but not on the disciplines of a life of holiness. There are churches that emphasize worship but spend a brief moment preaching through stories that reach the flesh but not the heart. Others prioritize the man-made doctrines of their denomination more than the solid theology written by the Spirit of God that was faithfully lived out by the early church.

A glass half empty will always leave room for the Enemy to fill it with worldly pleasures. That's why we need to teach the fullness of the gospel—so the message of Christ overflows in the hearts of those who listen to it.

It's true that the end of Paul's time in Ephesus ended with tears but not those of sadness. They were tears of hope, encouragement, and readiness for what's coming next. And what a scene the next one would be.

Following His Lead

Day 22

"A leader has a compass in his mind and a magnet in his heart."'
Vance Havner

"Then Paul answered, 'What are you doing, weeping and breaking my heart? For I am ready not only to be imprisoned but even to die in Jerusalem for the name of the Lord Jesus.'"

Acts 21:13

At this point in the book of Acts, Paul ventured his way back to Jerusalem, but not without both risk and warning. While the Holy Spirit prompted Paul in preparation for what was to come in the city, those around him were quick to keep him from traveling. Many people warned him about the dangers of going to Jerusalem. But in the midst of all the backlash from good-hearted followers of the Way, Paul felt an urgency to continue. He would soon discover that God wasn't stopping him from going to Jerusalem but preparing him for Jerusalem.

Day 22: Following His Lead

It's a lesson for us too. As Vance Habner said, every leader's mind is like a compass, showing us where to go. But they also have a heart that acts like a magnet. For Christians, our hearts are led by the Holy Spirit. Like a magnet, the Holy Spirit may interfere with our compass and where we are trying to go. While Paul got mixed messages from all the well-intended people around him, he still felt that still, small voice from the Holy Spirit—the voice directing him to *go*.

My question today for you is this: Where is your magnet telling you to go?

Interference

At the time, rumors started flying around Jerusalem about who precisely this Paul guy was. Many believed the rumor that he was an anti-Jewish person who encouraged others to be released from the law completely. They found his gospel message to be offensive and neglectful of Jewish law. Several others regarded him as a breaker of the law, someone with no regard for God's way.

On the contrary, Paul adhered to the law. He had even taken the Nazarite vow, the only vow that required him to shave his hair and offer three different offerings to show his dedication to the Jewish law. Despite all that, Paul believed the Gentiles didn't need to take a vow as he had before—but they *could*. He believed it was useless but not destructive.

At the same time, many Jews at the time were zealous for the law. They heard that Paul told the others to neglect the law, which was untrue. Paul believed Jews could still follow the laws—even he did in some regard—but following the law did not save them. Jesus was the only sacrifice needed for that.

The Revenant

Even still, how easy is it for good-intentioned Christians to be influenced by other good-intentioned Christians? And it's not like we shouldn't listen to those with wise counsel. Because I have been led and counseled by many strong and wise people in my life who helped me become who I am. What's most important, though, is to have such a strong relationship with the Lord that His voice is the loudest.

My first full-time job after being a part-time college pastor at Clemson for several years was at a church in Charleston, SC. It had a youth group of about eighty-five students, and it grew to almost four hundred students. This megachurch was terrific, and I was surrounded by dozens of wise mentors. Being new, I was really trying to get to know everyone. I connected with a fantastic leader at the church who happened to be the family pastor. Since I was newly hired, he had me and my wife, Amy, take a family psychology and giftings test to see how compatible we were. We had been married for quite a few years at the time and felt we were doing really well.

After taking the test, he called us into his office. We knew we were going to get a chance to analyze our giftings, discuss our incompatibilities, and be encouraged in our marriage.

That wasn't what happened.

The pastor looked at us with concern on his face and said, "These are some of the worst results I've ever seen on one of these tests. With almost one hundred percent accuracy, everyone who gets married with your personality types does not stay married."

Those words coming from an incredibly kind, wise, and God-loving person shocked us. How could this be? Were we really that incompatible?

"I have to warn you both," he said seriously. "Hardships and suffering are on the way."

That was twenty-five years ago.

Day 22: Following His Lead

Amy is my best friend. She was the love of my life when we first married at twenty years old and remains the love of my life today. Every date night, we drive to Beaufort, South Carolina, and make our way down the boardwalk hand in hand. We watch the sun slowly sneak its way below the horizon until it's completely engulfed in the water. Every now and then, Amy will bring a Bluetooth speaker, and we will dance slowly to eighties love songs, remembering where we've been and where we're going.

If we had listened to that good-intentioned pastor, we wouldn't have this tradition. If we had listened to that good-intentioned pastor, we would have never adopted our three biracial children, Malachi, Jeremiah, and Isaiah. If we had listened to that good-intentioned pastor, I wouldn't be where I am in my walk with the Lord today. Amy has been by my side every step of the way, always pointing me to Christ. She is such a testament to God's goodness to me.

It would have been easy for Paul to listen to those concerned and heartfelt pleas of the Christians who feared for his safety. But the Holy Spirit acted as a magnet to interfere with Paul's compass. As a result, he boldly continued to Jerusalem. He didn't allow someone else's prayer life to supersede his own.

We can follow his example today by rooting ourselves in our own relationship with God. When we focus on His voice speaking to us through the Holy Spirit, we can follow His perfect leading no matter where the compass seems to direct us.

Taken to the Rapids

As the angry mob continued to gather in Jerusalem in response to Paul, the Roman officials began to worry about all of the uproars. They decided to handcuff Paul to two Roman officials after being beaten and whipped for hours.

The Revenant

"Away with him!" they shouted but not away to jail or away from the city. Away to *death*.

He was sentenced to death because of his love of the gospel. Because of his commitment to the Holy Spirit's voice. Because of his boldness to speak out to the crowds.

In prison, Paul's limp and bruised body lay on the cold cell floor in chains. Everyone in the jail believed him to be a dangerous terrorist until they found out he was actually a citizen of Tarsus. Paul says, "I am a Jew, from Tarsus in Cilicia, a citizen of no obscure city. I beg you, permit me to speak to the people" (Acts 21:39).

It's hard not to get emotional as I reflect on Paul's fierce determination and heart for the Lord even when his situation seemingly couldn't get any worse. *Nothing*—not even being hated and facing death—was going to stop him from preaching the gospel. He knew that if the world hated him, it hated Jesus first (John 15:18).

Years ago, Amy and I were driving through the mountains while on vacation and enjoying the beautiful fall leaves. Along the way, we decided to stop at a small country store with crafts, sandwiches, and a beautiful view of the rapids overlooking the mountains.

As my wife looked through the crafts, I couldn't stop staring at the beautiful rapids.

"Does anyone ever go down those rapids?" I asked the cashier.

"It has been raining," she replied. "The rapids would be too dangerous for swimming with the strong current!"

We purchased our lunch and decided to sit on a picnic table next to the flowing rapids, sun shining brightly on our faces. But the rapids kept calling me.

Finally, I told Amy, "I'm jumping in the river. It's time to ride those rapids!"

Day 22: Following His Lead

"Are you serious?!" Amy responded, "She said it's too dangerous!"

"Well, I was water skiing on Lake Norman in Mooresville, North Carolina, when I was five years old. It's a good thing that I'm part fish," I replied.

With the confidence of a UFC cage fighter about to fight a five-round championship fight, I marched over to the river and removed my shoes and shirt. I was ready to jump in. For the first few seconds, I floated down the river peacefully. The icy cold water sent chills up my arms and legs, but I didn't care. It made me feel alive!

Those feelings soon changed, however, as I floated under a bridge and felt the river jolt me along a bit faster. I was no longer floating but was quickly being sucked down into the rapids. It felt like I was in a cup of water that someone was slurping with a straw. The force of the water slammed my body against the rocks under the water and scraped my back along the bottom. I thought I broke my tailbone. Just as I thought I couldn't hold my breath any longer, the rapids spit me onto a large boulder in the middle of the river.

I lay there for a second, gasping for air, trying to process what had just happened. Then, I slowly turned around and looked back at my wife. Everyone was staring at me in shock. Amy had her hands over her mouth, shaking her head embarrassingly. The warmth of the sun heated up the boulder, and I let my body melt against the sun and rock. Looking up in the sky, I couldn't help but think about how unbelievably peaceful I felt. Then, it got even better.

Small splashing noises made my ears perk up, and I sat up to find the source of the sound. There, right in the middle of the rapid, were rainbow trout jumping all around me as they caught the mosquitos above the water. The beautiful

~169~

fall leaves rustled in the wind as the sun shined brightly over God's creation.

The rainbow trout could not have been seen or heard from the bank eating my sandwich. They couldn't have been seen from inside the shop or from the car ride. No, the only place I could have experienced this beautiful moment was by going down the rough rapids.

At that moment, I heard the Holy Spirit whisper to me: *There's nothing wrong with having a sandwich on the bank of the river, but I've called you to be radical and jump in and ride the rapids.*

Paul knew how rough the rapids of following Christ could be. He was at rock bottom himself. In response to his request to speak to the mobs from jail, the guards obliged. Weak in body but strong in Spirit, Paul, still chained and disfigured, rose to his feet. He chose to speak in Hebrew to communicate with the Jews, not the Roman officials.

In following Christ, the road is rarely smooth, predictable, or straight. Oftentimes, following Christ can feel like that magnet interfering with our compass. But when we choose to embrace the Holy Spirit and swim through the rough rapids, God always arrives in time to meet us with his perfect presence and perfect plan.

Oh, and the message Paul delivered to the mobs of people? Well, you'll simply have to find out in the next chapter.

He Uses Us

ᗪAY 23

"If you give it to God, He transforms your test into a testimony, your mess into a message, and your misery into a ministry."
Rick Warren

"And one Ananias, a devout man according to the law, well spoken of by all the Jews who lived there, came to me, and standing by me said to me, 'Brother Saul, receive your sight.' And at that very hour I received my sight and saw him."

Acts 22:12-13

With eyes as red as their faces the crowd was seething with anger, like a bull ready to charge.

Paul stood among them ready to give his defense to the angry Jews, attempting every way he could to appeal to the crowd.

In Greek, the word *defense* is *apologia*, which means apologetic—not like saying you're sorry but a defense of why one believes something. And Paul didn't defend the gospel in a way the crowd might have expected. He chose to speak to the crowd

The Revenant

with something irrefutable—his testimony. In the presence of the angry mob who sought to kill Paul just moments before, he boldly shared the story of how Jesus found him. Paul shared about his conduct before Christ came to him, during his conversion, and throughout his commission by Christ.

Not only was Paul aware of the undeniable impact that God could have on the lives of believers, but he also knew how to artfully convey this truth to the crowd, creating a beautiful connection. And God chose to use that to reach the crowd.

God could have reached the crowd through angels, visions, or miracles. But instead he used Paul.

As we study Paul's testimony that he shared with the Jews in Jerusalem, let us be encouraged by the incredible power that God gives us through our own personal stories. Because while we know that God can reach and transform even those who seem lost or unreachable . . .

He still chooses to use us.

The Pattern in Acts

Like the talented communicator he was, Paul was able to eloquently relate to the crowd by exposing the persecution and terror he once brought on followers of the Way. He said, "I persecuted this Way to the death, binding and delivering into prisons both men and women" (v. 4). The crowd was most likely shocked by this, considering he was now willing to *be* persecuted for the Way. He was able to relate to the public because he once did the same thing. And even though he had been a Christian for several years now, he still understood those who were not.

Paul then shared his conversion story of how the Lord came to him on his way to Damascus. This was the moment that we studied in Acts 9, when Paul became blinded by the heavenly

Day 23: He Uses Us

light. The Lord said, " 'Saul, Saul, why are you persecuting me?' And he said, 'Who are You, Lord?' Then the Lord said, 'I am Jesus, whom you are persecuting' " (Acts 9:4-5). It's interesting that the Lord didn't introduce himself with any superior title, although he definitely had earned one. The Lord didn't introduce himself as sir or mister or master. He simply said that He was Jesus. He was not asking to be respected with any fancy titles. Instead, He asked Paul to give Him his entire life. He longs to be known by Paul—deeply known.

Jesus said, "Not everyone who says to me, 'Lord, Lord,' will enter the kingdom of heaven, but only the one who does the will of my Father who is in heaven . . . I will tell them plainly, 'I never knew you. Away from me, you evildoers!'" (Matthew 7:21, 23, NIV). Jesus made clear to Paul that Jesus calls us beyond being a part of the Christian religion or going to a specific church every Sunday or memorizing a certain Scripture or catechism. Jesus wants our hearts and our lives. And this message is one that Paul desperately wanted to communicate to the crowd through his testimony.

As he continued to share his conversion story, Paul told the crowd of Jews that when the great light from heaven shone around him, the Lord said, "'Rise, and go into Damascus, and there you will be told all that is appointed for you to do'" (Acts 22:10). And if you don't remember what happened after this great light, Paul went on to tell the crowd how God used an ordinary man named Ananias to bring him to Christ.

Yes, a person.

God used a person to play an instrumental role in Paul's conversion.

It says in Acts 9 that the Lord said to Ananias, "'Go! This man is my chosen instrument to proclaim my name to the Gentiles and their kings and to the people of Israel. I will show him how much he must suffer for my name.' So Ananias departed" (v. 15-17). Sure enough, Paul shared with the crowd how Ananias found him just as the Lord said he would. And from there, Paul was baptized.

See, there is a pattern in the book of Acts. One that is repeated throughout almost every chapter. **God uses people to reach people.**

God used Ananias to speak to Paul (Acts 9). The Ethiopian eunuch asked Philip about whom the Scriptures were referring in Isaiah, and that's when God used Philip to share the good news about Jesus. Later, along their way, the eunuch was baptized (Acts 8:26-40). God used Cornelius to speak to Peter about how God does not show favoritism to the Jews or Gentiles but loves every person who accepts him and does what is right (Acts 10:31-36). Bottom line? God uses people to reach people.

But if we're honest, it can get really easy for us to let the world get in the way of what God calls us to do. Our lives are filled with work obligations, money pressure, childcare, health issues, relational stress, the list goes on. In our everyday lives we have to fight hard for God's work to gain priority on our to-do lists. But Paul reminded us in his message to the Jews that we can't let the world get in the way of what God has called us to do. Like a day of spring cleaning in a messy garage, we must make room in our hearts for the Lord, clearing out the unimportant and making room for the eternal.

That's when He can use you—which means that tomorrow could be the most exciting day of your life! Truly, the possibilities are endless when you think about the many ways God can use your story to change the lives of others. We simply must be obedient to the Lord's call, and He will use us.

Your very own Paul could be waiting for you to share God's love. After all, staunch Jews thought that Gentiles were used to flame the fires of hell to make it even hotter and more unbearable. But Paul accepted the Lord's mission of sharing the message of salvation with the Gentiles. Imagine what He has in store for you and those you meet.

The World

It was a hot day as I finished practicing my golf swing for an hour or so at the driving range. On my way out, I ran into an elderly man who worked at the range part-time. As we exchanged greetings, he shared with me that his wife had been diagnosed with osteoporosis and had broken so many bones that he would have to quit his job to take care of her. He even mentioned that she might never walk again.

Once hearing this, it didn't take me long to call the women at the church I was serving as a staff pastor at the time to start a meal train for his wife. People at our church could sign up to cook meals for the couple to take the burden off dinner during this difficult time. And the church showed up. Weeks' worth of food was set to be delivered to the couple, providing relief and the love of Christ to this family.

But anytime the world touches anything of God, it waters it down. One person at the church caught wind of the food ministry making meals for a couple who didn't attend our church. She refused to make any meals because the protocol was not to cook food for people without permission from the elders. Sometimes even the church can get so administrative and legalistic that we can't even cook a meal for someone in need.

Just as it can be tempting to allow the everyday stress of our lives to take over our commitment to the gospel, it can be tempting to let the world intervene too. The world has a tricky way of taking the gospel and making it weak.

The Revenant

You might remember hearing about the Asbury University revival in Wilmore, Kentucky, in 2023. This nonstop, two-week prayer session at the school brought tens of thousands of people, mostly Generation Z students, across the country to worship. People were praying, crying, singing, and worshiping together in the auditorium.

But as the world does, it takes a powerful revival like this and waters it down. After two weeks, university leaders commanded a stop to the revival. They wanted students to return to a normal academic schedule and stop the traffic in the city. And just like that, the revival was over.

Years ago, I actually spoke at Asbury University at a large Christian conference. I spoke on a side stage and was the emcee for the main stage event. At the time, the next step expected of me in my ministry career was to be trained in seminary, but God had other plans.

As a nondenominational evangelist, God has given me opportunities to tell people about the richness of the gospel every single day. I don't have to water it down or be confined to the parameters of a certain denomination. No, I get to preach the Bible every day, live and learn by experience, and share the gospel with anyone the Lord puts in my path. And truthfully, I cannot imagine living any other life. Every step of the way, the Lord gives me a chance to share my faith and love others in different ways. And every morning, I wake up with a fresh mindset of what God will do.

Like Paul, I get to be a vessel of the Lord's love and grace in a world full of brokenness. The best part is, God calls you to do this too. Whether you're a preacher or a teacher, a doctor or an artist, a stay-at-home mom, or a server, your career or life experience is irrelevant. God uses us.

He uses *you*.

Day 23: He Uses Us

We can trust that He will work in and through us to reach those that need Him most.

Sands of Providence

Day 24

"When you saw only one set of footprints, it was then that I carried you."

Flora Haines Loughead

"The following night the Lord stood by [Paul] and said, 'Take courage, for as you have testified to the facts about me in Jerusalem, so you must testify also in Rome.'"

Acts 23:11

There's a famous poem written in the 1800s by a woman named Flora Haines Loughead called *Footprints in the Sand*. You've probably heard it or seen a quote or two from this poem accompanied by a picture of footprints in the sand. It is written from the point of view of a person at the end of life, looking back at all the footprints of her and the Lord throughout her life. She notices that during the most difficult parts of her life, there was only one set of footprints. When she asked the Lord why this was, "He whispered, 'My precious child, I love you and will never leave

Day 24: Sands Of Providence

you. Never, ever, during your trials and testings. When you saw only one set of footprints, It was then that I carried you."

Both in the Bible and in our own lives, there are times when God makes many things happen, but we don't recognize or know that it is taking place at the time. That's called providence. Providence happens when you think you're alone in the sand, but unbeknownst to you, God was holding you.

Chapter 23 shows much of God's providence in Paul's journey. It's kind of like the book of Esther where her whole harrowing story was told but does not mention God at all. However, it is completely devoted to the providence of God behind the scenes.

As Luke writes this chapter of Acts, there is a steady theme: The Lord calls Paul to spread the gospel to the Gentiles throughout Asia and in Rome, and Paul suffers persecution along the way.

Yet in the midst of these disheartening events, God's providence remains constant.

DISAGREEMENT

When Paul addressed the crowd again, he got off to a rocky start. He addressed them as "men and brethren," probably because he used to be one of them (v.1). He also claimed that he had a clear conscience. For this comment, Paul was struck on the mouth. See, when Peter and Stephen addressed the Sanhedrin, they addressed the crowd as "elders and fathers" (Acts 4 and 7). Paul's remarks could have been interpreted by the Sanhedrin in many different ways, but it clearly shook Paul to the core when he was slapped immediately because he exploded in anger at being struck and scolded them for striking an innocent man. While Paul was justified in his reaction, he quickly realized he was wrong in the way he said it. He didn't realize that Ananias, the high priest, commanded him to be slapped. One should never speak poorly of a high priest in public, no matter how corrupt he is.

Paul's apology for acting out in the flesh should give us all comfort because how many times have we done this too? Jesus said to turn the other cheek (Matthew 5:39), but it's not always that easy.

I heard a story the other day about an Irish evangelist who was also an ex-boxer. One day, he was setting up a tent for a revival when a few drunks approached the tent and threatened him. Suddenly, one of the men struck the Irishman on the side of the face. He said nothing and simply stuck out his jaw. The other man then struck him on the other side of the face. That's when the Irish evangelist said, "The Lord gave me no further instructions!" and knocked them both out.

As funny as that story is, Paul wrote "We work hard, toiling with our own hands. When people abuse and insult us, we respond with a blessing, and when severely persecuted, we endure it" (1 Corinthians 4:12, NIV). As anyone who has been insulted knows, it's easier to act like the Irishman than how Jesus calls us to act. I mean, even after Paul wrote those words, he reacted negatively to the slap and had to ask for grace.

As he continued to speak, Paul cleverly decided to mention the resurrection of Jesus. With both Sadducees and Pharisees in the crowd, another riot broke out. See, he knew that the Pharisees could find common ground with him on this subject whereas the Sadducees did not believe in the resurrection, angels, or the Spirit.

Paul hoped that the Pharisees would talk to the Sadducees for him, but at the mention of the resurrection, the crowd went wild. These two parties fighting reminds me a lot of what's going on in our churches and political parties today. We've discussed numerous disagreements —petty ones that take away from the

Day 24: Sands Of Providence

ultimate goal of the church—within churches in this book already. And who doesn't know about the divide our country has over politics and political agendas.

Perhaps the biggest takeaway from this section of chapter 23 is not to let these petty things prevent you from sharing the gospel. Even with Paul's errors, he never allowed disagreements to stop him. We will shortly see how God honored him for that. Because once the crowd started going wild over Paul's words, it looked like he was going to be torn to shreds. That's when the soldiers took him to the barracks to keep him safe, and it's where we will see that God appears to Paul once again.

Alone, Afraid, Abandoned

Darkness often serves as Satan's covert refuge. A place where he thrives among the realms of loneliness, fear, and doubt. He loves to prey on individuals who are suffering, who perceive that they are alone in life and without any options.

I can think of many dark times in my life when I've felt this way, especially before I truly committed my life to Christ in that Pontiac Firebird all those years ago. Most recently, however, I remember a time in my family's life when we were met with confusion, sadness, and disappointment.

As you know by now, God sent me to Bluffton, South Carolina, for eight months to help rebuild a struggling church. When I first came to Bluffton, both of my sons were in their senior year of high school. The church was growing, and it looked like we were ready to move from my small two-bedroom condo into a new house in the Malind Bluff neighborhood in Okatie, South Carolina. In our thirty-four years together, my wife and I have lived in several different houses. None were super nice or special but made fine

~ 181 ~

The Revenant

enough homes considering the salary I made as a pastor. We have great memories in each home. But after all these years, we truly felt like God was providing us the opportunity to buy our dream home. Excitedly, we began scouring the area looking for nice homes to buy or ones to build.

One day, we drove into a newly developed neighborhood in Okatie with a few different model homes. If you've ever been to the Lowcountry of South Carolina, then you can imagine the vibes this neighborhood gave us. The marshes and coastal waterways were breathtaking, framed with old oak trees and Spanish moss. Many of the homes had charming oil lanterns burning at the entrance to welcome guests.

Above all the different floor plans this neighborhood had to offer were perfect. My wife fell in love with the Charleston Continental Home. This house exhibited an Old South feel, complete with everything from my wife's hand-selected countertops to the flooring. It was her dream home, and we were set to buy it.

While we waited for the home to be finished, I continued to live in my small two-bedroom condo with my mother who is in the late stages of dementia. After a couple of months of waiting, the builder reluctantly told us that they were running a bit behind.

"How behind?" we asked.

"About nine months," he responded.

Nine months?!

There was no way we could all live in my tiny condo for that long. We would have to buy another home. My wife was absolutely crushed. This was something she had been praying about for months, and she really felt like God was calling us there. It seemed like everything had come together only to fall apart.

Day 24: Sands Of Providence

Without another option, I asked my realtor to pull up some more houses for us. He informed us he wanted us to see a certain house in the same beautiful neighborhood where the other house fell through.

"We already had a house there that we wanted, and it's not ready. We're not really interested in any of the other style homes available," I warned.

My realtor replied, "Let's just give it a shot in case."

We agreed and drove through the neighborhood again looking longingly at the Spanish moss and oak trees. When we came up to the home, we couldn't believe our eyes.

It was the Charleston Continental. The exact home we wanted, complete with every upgrade from the screened-in back porch to the oil lantern on the front patio. We were able to move in within two weeks. It's as though God said, "Your way was nine months. My way is two weeks."

God's providence.

To top it all off, we have had the opportunity to get to know our neighbors and minister to many of them already. We've befriended the ones right next door to us, and it so happens they were looking for a church.

God's providence.

After a year of living in this amazing home, we had our one-year inspection. After the inspector finished, he came to me and said, "Christian, I have to be honest. I do the inspections on most of the houses in the neighborhood, and a huge percentage of the homes have a lot wrong with them. But yours..." his voice trailed off. "The other houses had the D team build their homes. Yours was built by the A team. There's absolutely nothing wrong with your home."

God's providence.

When we got that call from the builder originally, it felt as though we were all alone. God didn't hear. Or if he did, he said no. But as the Lord's providence works, sometimes you can't see God's footprints because he's been holding you in his arms the entire time.

When Paul was in the barracks, he, too, was alone but not alone. The very same prison Paul was in was the prison Peter was in where the doors swung open, and he was freed! The doors, however, stay providentially closed for Paul. It would be the same gospel spread, but by a different route. In the depths of despair, Jesus stood by Paul in prison and said, "'Take courage, for as you have testified to the facts about me in Jerusalem, so you must testify also in Rome'" (Acts 23:11). The Lord told Paul that there was more for him to do!

In our darkness and loneliness, God knows what we need to hear and when we need to hear it. Paul *needed* to hear that he would be going to Rome. He *needed* to hear that there would be protection for tomorrow. And boy, did he get the protection he needed. Like an exaggeration of the Lord's faithfulness, Paul was escorted out of prison by 470 trained Roman soldiers to await trial by Felix in Caesarea—further proof that God takes care of his people to completion.

And just as God's promise was fulfilled and sticking to the theme of the chapter, Felix waited for the governor who wanted to speak to Paul. He went on to spend two years in confinement in Herod's Praetorium and another two years in Rome under Felix's custody. God's providence following him the entire way.

Today and every day, you are walking through the sands of your own life, sometimes leaping and other times being carried. Maybe right now, you're in a season where God doesn't seem to be listening. This chapter begs us to remember that while currently time may seem to be at a standstill, you will one day look back at the sands of your life and see the footprints of God's providence every step of the way.

The Killer of Tens of Thousands

Day 25

"When you're with God, one is the majority."
Martin Luther

"But this I confess to you, that according to the Way, which they call a sect, I worship the God of our fathers, believing everything laid down by the Law and written in the Prophets."

Acts 24:14

Not too long ago, I heard a story from a local pastor about a new family that moved into town. When he found out this family didn't have a church home, he invited them to visit his church down the street. Reluctantly, the husband said, "I don't know if I really want to, but maybe one day when I get my life straightened out, I'll come visit."

A few months later, the pastor ran into the same man. Again, the pastor invited the man to church. And again, the man said, "Pastor, I just don't have my life straightened out yet."

A couple of weeks later, the man died. Everyone wondered if he was a Christian, and the pastor said, "I'm not sure. But he was a man of his word. Look at him in the casket. He's defintiely straightened out." Sadly, the man procrastinated on Christ for so long that he waited for rigor mortis to straighten his life out, which is exactly what it does.

This story accurately identifies a large majority of the church today. The Pareto principle states that 80 percent of work is done by 20 percent of people. Think of that statistic in terms of the modern church. Twenty percent of congregants serve throughout the week. Twenty percent of congregants radically share their testimony. Twenty percent of the congregants attend regularly, tithe consistently, pray daily, and tap into the word beyond Sunday mornings.

And if you want the truth, people who faithfully give to the church are actually a much smaller percentage than twenty. In the last five churches that I've been a part of, less than 5 percent of the congregation gave regularly to the church.

In this chapter of Acts, we will read about some procurators who oversaw the trials of Paul and who seemed to have killed thousands before him. However, we will learn about something they did that killed way more than thousands. It's the same thing that's killing tens of thousands of people in the modern-day church too.

Procrastination.

The Thief of Time

At Paul's trial, his accusers called him many names. They found him to be a plague who stirred up riots and pegged him as the ringleader of the Nazarenes (which, by the way, is the only time the New Testament uses that term to define

Day 25: The Killer Of Tens Of Thousands

Christians—a derogatory word). They weren't calling Paul anything good, even though he was following God's call for his life as a faithful Christian.

If you've been in the church for any time, you can probably relate to being labeled because of what you believe. So, what is it that they call you?

Do they find you a procrastinating Christian who lives a life of complacency? One who goes to church every so often? A good person? A person who goes to their kids' baseball games and vacations in the summer? Are you a person radical in posting about your political beliefs online but not as radical in sharing your testimony?

All too often, modern churchgoers sit complacently, as if waiting for a better time to share the gospel. We put off reading our Bible for tomorrow when something better comes up today. We feel prompted to share our testimony but choose to let the time pass in fear of seeming different. Maybe we even put off taking our kids to church because of worldly tasks that seem more important. It's this procrastination and complacency that kills the church today. But we don't have to accept that as the norm.

When we look at Paul in the midst of the slow-moving people who oversaw trials at the time, we get a clear look at the antithesis of procrastination. If Paul needed to do something, he didn't put it off or make excuses. He simply *did* it. There was a time in his life when he needed an income, but he didn't want to take it from the church, so he started making tents for a living. He did whatever needed to be done to make the church prosper, and he did it immediately. And even at this point in Acts, after all the trials and pressure of growing the church, Paul continued to preach.

In fact, it says in verse 10 that he cheerfully made his defense. In Greek, *cheerfully* means "in fine spirits." There is truly a spirit-filled life when Christ is your Savior. But as the world does, it takes what God deems holy and corrupts it.

During the COVID-19 lockdown, do you remember what was left open after almost everything else was closed? Liquor stores. The liquor stores were left open to fill the spirits of the world and take away the spirit of life that propels the ministry of the gospel. Meanwhile, the churches were shut down, preventing people from sharing the gospel in fine spirits as Paul did. Instead of persisting in sharing the gospel, the church sat complacent in the hands of the government.

Again, this doesn't have to be our norm. During Paul's speech in front of the governor and all his accusers, he capitalized on every moment he had. He didn't hesitate to clearly defend himself. You see, Paul knew he wasn't a troublemaker. He lived with honesty and integrity. When you're living with integrity, you don't have to be slick or misleading. You just have to be precise and honest. With the help of the Holy Spirit, Paul made his defense, and God's providence was before him.

The procurator Felix was known to be a brutally cruel individual, yet he decided to allow Paul, as a free man, to receive others and get help from them while he was held. Even in his cruel nature, Felix was controlled by God, so Paul was given permission to pray and share the gospel.

This is what can happen when we use the time that's given to us to obey God's call on our lives. As Proverbs says, "Don't put it off; do it now! Don't rest until you do" (Proverbs 6:4, NLT). In this section of Acts we are reminded that we only have a set number of days on earth to fulfill our divine purpose. So let us refrain from allowing our precious time to be stolen by procrastination. Instead, let us strive to be energetic for God's kingdom while the days are still here.

Day 25: The Killer Of Tens Of Thousands

Stand Firm

The other day I was listening to the Joe Rogan podcast with guest Matthew McConaughey. The famous American actor was sharing his testimony. In the interview, McConaughey shares that he is a man of faith and believes in the Bible but doesn't know what to do with the magic tricks. He was referring to the miracles in the Old Testament like Noah's Ark, Jonah and the whale, and so on.

Many modern-day people who refer to themselves as Christians share McConaughey's stance on these "magic tricks." Instead of calling themselves atheists, they claim they have spirituality. They simply don't know how to believe in the stories of the Bible, so they believe they are folktales passed down to teach a lesson.

Joe Rogan himself felt similarly about Bible stories like Noah's Ark. In fact, in one of his comedy shows, Rogan makes his point clearly with a rather offensive joke. He jokes that if you were to tell a mentally slow eight-year-old boy the story of Noah's Ark, even he would tell the storyteller that he just made that up.

Clearly, many spiritual people dismiss half of the Bible, yet still claim to be Christians. They make assumptions and claims about certain beliefs, ideas, and people that may or may not align with Christianity. And before you know it, they've completely left the faith because of their perceived beliefs rather than relying on the Bible's truth.

Admittedly, one of my biggest irritations is when I hear Christians say that a certain political party or denomination is the problem with the church. I (and many other pastors) have experienced members of the church dividing over political conversations. Once, I had a family I had been faithfully ministering to leave my church to return to Catholicism when he

The Revenant

heard me talk about how Martin Luther confronted the Catholic Church because they were telling people they could buy their deceased loves ones out of hell. He shared with me over the phone that he was taught to hate Martin Luther because he started the Great Reformation, and if he had not started this revival that led to the exodus of many in the Catholic Church the whole world would be Catholic today. I guess he missed the part where Luther went underground and translated the Bible from Latin to English so that people could read it. He helped the church honor God in how they lived.

During Paul's defense, he testified about his faith because he firmly believed in the Old Testament. He said that he believed everything "laid down by the Law and written in the Prophets" (Acts 24:14). His faith was solidified by those stories not broken down by them. In fact, Paul claimed that the stories in the Old Testament brought *clarity* and *assurance* to his faith.

What about you? Do you believe in creation? The worldwide flood? The book of Genesis? The plagues in Egypt? The parting of the Red Sea? The world likes to pick and choose what best fits their unique spirituality, but Paul never did that. He never compromised or procrastinated in his faith.

The church's greatest enemies are not Democrats or Republicans. They aren't Martin Luther or the Pope. The greatest enemy is the complacency of people who say they love Christ.

After Joe Rogan makes his joke about the ridiculousness of the story of Noah's Ark, he goes backstage and is told by one of his assistants that an archaeologist who found remnants of Noah's Ark wanted to come back stage and talk to him about his joke. Shocked, but always ready for a good debate, Joe Rogan had his assistant lead the archaeologist back to his dressing room where the archaeologist asked Rogan, "I mean, what do you do when you find a boat that matches the dimensions in the Bible? And it's six-thousand-year-old wood?"

Many years after this encounter, Rogan had two scientists on his podcast that gave data to prove there was, in fact, a worldwide flood. A man who previously spent ten years making fun of it is now a firm believer in it!

It can be tempting to be hard-headed toward the Bible and procrastinate for years before finally having faith. When Felix heard Paul's defense, one translation says that he trembled after Paul preached. Paul was able to reason with the Word. D. L. Moody says that if you throw a rock at a pack of dogs, the one that got hit is the one yelping. The same thing goes for powerful and reasonable messages. Felix was hit by the truth, and you could tell. Like the dog, he was yelping and conflicted in his life.

But Felix? He chose to walk away. He chose procrastination, which we now know kills tens of thousands.

So I think the question to end the chapter is this: What will you do? Will you wait to let someone else carry on the divine work God has laid out for you, letting the thief of time steal your call? Or will you embrace the truth of the gospel, pray for belief in your unbelief, and stand firm in what God says? I believe you know what to do. And I also pray that God will give you the strength you need to resist being a Felix.

Perils of Placating

DAY 26

"You can please some people some of the time, all people some of the time, some people all of the time, but you can never please all people all of the time."

Abraham Lincoln

"Paul argued in his defense, 'Neither against the law of the Jews, nor against the temple, nor against Caesar have I committed any offense.'"

Acts 25:8

It had been two years since Paul was first brought before Felix. Two years of the Jews' hostility toward the gospel. Two years since Paul gave his defense to Antonius Felix and was confined under Claudius. Two years since the trial in Caesarea and being thrown out of court.

Two years later, people still harbored hatred in their hearts against a man that continued to show unconditional love. However, little did Paul know, his two-year confinement in

Day 26: Perils Of Placating

Caesarea proved to be a providential grace from God. It meant rest from the previous years of travel and persecution and protection from the religious leaders who wanted him dead.

This time, Paul would be going on trial again in Caesarea, but under a different governor: Festus. He was appointed by Caesar to be the governor for two years after Felix's reign. Again, Paul found himself in the same boat, undergoing the same questions he did two years prior under Felix. If I had to guess, Paul was probably loving giving his defense to all these governors.

So who was this new governor? If Felix was the procrastinator, then Festus was the placater—something just as dangerous as a procrastinator. He strived to appease or modify his own thoughts and ideas to meet the interest or expectations of others. In essence, a placater changes him or herself to please another. Throughout the chapter and the history of the Roman governors, we see a pattern of placating that results in destruction. But Paul bravely and consistently stood with the Lord no matter what kind of opposition he faced.

A Bloodline Of Sin

While Felix, the predecessor to Festus, was known as a cruel and evil governor, Festus was generally a good governor. He governed with justice and wisdom despite Felix's mistakes. But prior to Festus' governorship, Judea had a history of sin and placating others.

King Agrippa II's father was King Herod, the one who had James beheaded and ordered Peter to be killed until God stepped in. Herod's grandfather was the one who beheaded John the Baptist and had his head brought to him on a platter. Before that, Agrippa II's great-grandfather was the one who killed all the babies in Bethlehem trying to stop the birth of Jesus. Agrippa I was struck down by the Lord and eaten by worms "because he did not give God glory" (Acts 12: 23).

Not only was Agrippa II's family before him entrenched in sin, but his own sister kept the cycle going as well. Bernice was Agrippa II's sister. Roman historian Josephus says their relationship was incestuous. King after king, father after father, this family created a legacy of dishonor, continuously reaping destruction on the church. No one seemed to change in the family line even when they had the chance.

I wonder how much of this placating to others is just as problematic today as it was all those years ago in Judea. How much of this continuous resistance to change still occurs in the modern church? Or within the four walls of our homes?

If we're honest, it's often easier to submit to people's preferences than to change our own for who God needs us to be.

Maybe you held out on inviting someone to your small group because the dynamic is good the way it is. It's easier to keep the status quo rather than risking discomfort. Perhaps you felt called to ministry but chose a more practical route in order to please your family. It's easier to choose security rather than taking a leap of faith. It could be that your church decided to invest thousands of dollars on a professional production rig to entertain guests rather than spending thousands on those in need. It's easier to prioritize the happiness of those inside the building rather than those on the outside.

Or maybe your church refuses to change at all. What worked for a hundred years still works for those in attendance. Placating to your current congregation sure is easier and more comfortable than changing to engage others after all.

Like those wicked Judean rulers following the same road for generation after generation simply taking the road they've always taken is easier than carving out a new path from God's

Day 26: Perils Of Placating

calling. Imagine what could have been if one of those Judean leaders would have stopped the injustice and persecution. Think about what could have been if one of them submitted to the Lord and received his blessing. What impact would that have made on history?

God's plan always goes beyond the what ifs. But it is worth pondering whether the history of placating in Judea might linger in the modern-day church.

How many present-day husbands struggle to stay in a marriage because they never had a good role model? How many women endure toxicity and abuse in relationships because they, too, never knew anything different? What about churchgoers who pop into church on major holidays only because that's what their families raised them to do? Or the sports teams, universities, and business owners that have terrible leaders year after year? Their teams lose, their profits take a hit, and ultimately those places close down. When we don't change the cycle, the cycle repeats.

A couple of weeks ago, I was invited to a tent revival in Myrtle Beach, South Carolina. Stepping into the event felt like a journey back in time, reminiscent of an era when sawdust covered the ground beneath the giant circus tent. The aroma of cotton candy, peanuts, and food trucks filled the air as the speakers warmly welcomed the crowd. People came from all walks of life—families with children, people who curiously spotted the tent off the side street, and even those seeking permanent shelter or grappling with addiction.

The man introducing everyone onstage was well built and reminded me of Richard Gere with salt and pepper hair. As I approached the director of the event, I asked who the man was. She beamed, "Oh, he's the pastor of the large church next door. He used to be a Chippendale striptease dancer before he came to Christ."

I laughed with joy, loving to hear how this man leading a community to Christ broke the cycle of sin in his story. Half an hour later, I noticed another man walking around, praying for people.

"What about him?" I asked the director.

"He's another pastor that's sponsoring the event tonight. He used to be a Hell's Angels Enforcer."

My jaw dropped as I recalled the days my dad was a professional flat track racer. Every year at Daytona during Bike Week, the championship race was held. My dad and other racers would rub elbows and party with the Hell's Angels and the Outlaw biker gangs. I knew an enforcer was the baddest of the bad and an individual you only bumped into once before the lights permanently shut off. It absolutely blew my mind to think about how the very people who put their hands on people to take a life were now putting their hands on others to give life in the name of Jesus. Another cycle of sin broken; another life committed to the kingdom of God.

As I kept looking around the tent, I noticed a joyful young woman bouncing around, serving people with a smile, bursting with positivity and energy.

"And this person?" I asked.

"Before coming to Christ, she was so deep in depression that she attempted suicide. But now, she's one of the most cheerful volunteers we have," the director explained.

Each and every one of these people refused to placate to the hand they were dealt. They didn't let their environment or their family history dictate their decisions or beliefs. Like Paul, they chose to find their true identity in Christ and make a difference in the lives of others.

You see, nothing productive ever comes from placating. But when we discover who we are, we don't have to change for anyone. We can be confident that God will work through us and make a way.

What Could Have Been Should Not Have Been

When Saul of Tarsus was younger, he thought he would be a Rabbi in Jerusalem and be on the ruling council of the Sanhedrin. He was actually trained under the great teacher Gamielel, a leading authority in the Sanhedrin in the early first century, and believed his path was meant for leadership in Jerusalem. But as we know, that's not what happened. God had other plans for young Saul, and his journey took a drastic turn.

My story started in a similar way. While playing baseball down the road from Clemson, my mentor John Reeves started a church at the Esso Bar and Grille. Before he became my mentor, I went to an FCA meeting where he was speaking. To this day, that message still rings in my ears and was probably one of the most influential moments that led me to be a pastor. There were over a thousand people there, and the message was about freedom in the spirit. He shared that having a relationship with Christ is powerful and life changing. I had never heard a message like this in my small, hometown Wesleyan church. John spoke with such power and authority, and I felt God's Spirit in that moment like never before.

After the sermon, I approached John and said, "I don't know what you have, but I want it."

From there John decided to invest in me. His small invitation to meet him at Keith Street Bar and Grille every Tuesday to disciple me was the ticket to my life in ministry. Every Tuesday after class and before baseball practice, I would meet with him at

The Revenant

that small restaurant for a whole year. With each conversation, story, and prayer, he slowly cracked me out of my Wesleyan shell.

You see, I had every intention of being a Wesleyan pastor. But the more I talked to John, the more I grew to love him and the way he ministered to people. My discipleship with John grew into acts of service around the community, helping freshmen move into their dorms, baptizing people in Lake Hartwell, feeding the homeless, ministering to people at bars, and inviting them to church the next day. My heart was growing more and more in love with this thing called ministry. And I felt God leading me somewhere amazing.

During this extraordinary time, I was also traveling and singing with a duet group called Heart and Soul with a good friend of mine, Scott Wheeler. We were traveling and getting enough opportunities that I started wondering if my calling was to be a worship leader. I would write and perform Christian music and make that my ministry.

One day, we were singing at a youth camp close to Clemson University where John lived. I invited him to come hear us perform. We sang, gave our testimonies, and ministered to the young people. On stage, I beamed with pride as I thought about what John must be thinking seeing me shine for the Lord. I was leading worship and impacting lives. What could be better than that?

After the performance, I asked John what he thought of the concert, and he simply stated, "Yeah, it was alright. But you're not called to sing, you're called to preach." And then he walked away.

John's reaction shook me to my core. His words wounded me and quite frankly, made me angry. I felt I was good at leading praise and worship. I loved music, and I knew I could make an impact for the gospel by doing this.

Day 26: Perils Of Placating

Paul, too, thought he knew what his future held. He was educated by the best of the best. He could have done *huge* things being a Rabbi. But God had other plans. Paul didn't placate to what his younger dreams were or what anyone else thought for him. He listened to the Lord, who said he would speak to the Gentiles even though he knew nothing. It wouldn't be through his own wisdom but through the Lord's.

Music could have been a good path for me. But at that moment, John didn't let me placate. He reminded me of the first time I spoke at his church Downtown Community Fellowship in Clemson, South Carolina, to over five hundred college students. He reminded me how there was an anointing there that night. If it wasn't for John's honesty and Spirit-filled gift, who knows where I would be now? God used John to keep me on track. And my life of preaching the gospel has filled my life with more joy and favor than I ever thought possible.

What *could have been* in my life was not what *should have been*.

What *could have been* for Paul was not what *should have been*.

What *could be* for you may not be what *should be*.

Like Paul, you have the ability to reflect on your life—past, present, and future—and ask the Lord who he would have you be. What cycle in your family will stop with you in the name of Jesus? Who would the Lord have you minister to in your circle of influence this year? How can you quit placating to others in your job, friendship, or relationships?

It's not an easy task, this spiritual work. Trust me, I know. Sometimes it will take someone saying "you're alright" for the Lord to get his point across.

But rest assured, the less you focus on what others believe *could be*, the more you can direct your gaze to what *is* and *is to come* in the life we have in Jesus.

Freedom in Chains

Day 27

"As God is consistent in His pursuit of us, our return of that pursuit brings us to spiritual maturity."
Lynn Cowell

"And Paul said, 'Whether short or long, I would to God that not only you but also all who hear me this day might become such as I am—except for these chains.'"

Acts 26:29

Time and time again, we have read throughout the book of Acts how Paul used his platform to share his own personal testimony. Whether it was on the floor of a jail cell or on a podium in chains, Paul never wavered in his dedication to the gospel. In chapter 26, Paul got the chance to plead his case against Agrippa and Festus.

As mentioned before, Agrippa's family history was absolutely stacked against Jesus. His great-grandfather tried to murder Jesus as a baby, his grandfather had John the Baptist beheaded,

Day 27: Freedom In Chains

and his father killed James because of his belief in Jesus. With this kind of history, it was unlikely Agrippa would see Paul's side. But that doesn't stop Paul from passionately and respectfully communicating his message to him.

See, Paul knew clearly what his call from Jesus was. He was laser-focused on being a minister, a servant of things seen and yet to be seen. He was also called to bear witness and experience the call of being a Christian. And even though this meant being in chains, Paul was always more interested in telling people about freedom in Jesus than freeing himself.

A Solid Foundation

As we imagine Paul pleading his case and sharing his testimony to Agrippa and Festus, I want you to picture Paul's appearance as described by Onesiphorus, a personal friend of Paul. He says that Paul was a "man small in stature, with a bald head and crooked legs, in good state of body, with eyebrows that meet and a nose that is somewhat hooked, full of friendliness; for now he appeared like a man, and now he had the face of an angel."[8] Onesiphorus communicated how Paul spoke with such joy and confidence even though he was in chains, and even though he was not the most attractive man. Paul encapsulated what Peter wrote: "Always be prepared to make a defense to anyone who asks you for the reason for the hope that is in you; yet do it with gentleness and respect" (1 Peter 3:15).

Just as Jesus did before him, Paul turned his trial to a testimony and his opposition into opportunity. And his vigilance and oversight in sharing his testimony should encourage us to be ready too. Think about it. When Jesus met the woman at the well,

---

[8] E. Hennecke, W. Schneemelcher, R .McL. Wilson (ed.), *New Testament Apocrypha*, E.T., ii London, 1965, pp. 353 f.v

she was there to draw water, but Jesus led her to a story about living water. When Jesus fed the hungry crowd in Galilee, he then led them into a conversation about the bread of life (John 6:22-59). In every conversation Jesus had, he was prepared to share the love of the gospel.

When I think about Paul's story, I remember that when he gave his life to Jesus, he couldn't have been more educated in the faith. He went away for three years to be discipled by the Holy Spirit before sharing the gospel for the rest of his life. In order to fulfill God's call on his life, he had to develop a strong foundation of faith.

Similarly, when my wife and I were raising our three boys, we knew we wanted them to grow up with that same foundation Paul had. That's why we decided to send them to a Christian school so that they would feel prepared and ready to walk with Jesus through adulthood. Today, I have three grown sons. Malachi is in the Army. Isaiah is studying business at Liberty University. And Jeremiah is in the Marine Corps. All three of them are walking with Jesus and ministering to others in the place God put them, and I could not be more proud as a father.

When Isaiah was a sophomore at Liberty he became one of the youngest resident assistants they've ever had. RAs are typically given to juniors or seniors, but they saw something different about Isaiah. They noticed his integrity and maturity, which only can be attested to the Holy Spirit. When he told me why he wanted to be an RA, he said that the role would allow him to have conversations about Jesus with the residents on the floor and make a positive impact on their lives. Sharing the gospel with others is a foundational part of who Isaiah is, and I believe that is because of the way he was raised.

God led my son Jeremiah to the Marine Corps. When he was away at boot camp, I wasn't able to contact him, so I reached out

Day 27: Freedom In Chains

to a connection I had with a chaplain at Parris Island to see if I could get an update. When I got in touch, the chaplain informed me that Jeremiah was a squad leader (there are only four in a platoon), and tons of Marines were hearing the Word of God through him! Apparently, during their one hour of free time, Jeremiah started a Bible study and invited other Marines to join.

Malachi is in the Army and scored extremely high on his entry test. He got into a branch of the Army with lots of intellectual people who often pull away from the faith and are lost. But Malachi continues to go to the three-hour chapel service every Sunday and unashamedly shares his faith with his Army buddies. Without his strong foundation of faith, it would be incredibly challenging for Malachi to stand strong in the Word of God. His faith is grounding him, and he's already begun to see fruit from the conversations he is having with his Army friends.

Hearing how my boys are active and strong in their faith into adulthood brings tears to my eyes because I remember.

I remember parenting them when they were growing up, and the struggle at times to prioritize God over anything else. I remember when Jeremiah desperately wanted to play AAU basketball and games were on Sundays. We told him he couldn't play because my wife and I weren't willing to sacrifice the time our family had on Sundays to gather in the Lord's house with our community. That was too important, and basketball was not going to take precedence over that. I remember how mad he was at us, and how long it took him to understand our reasoning.

I remember how they couldn't get a phone until they were sixteen. No social media until eighteen. They were allowed only one hour of video games per week. From the time they were sixteen, they always had to have a part-time job during school and a full-time job during summer.

The Revenant

I remember how the choices and boundaries my wife and I set were not always popular in our parenting circle. Even Christian parents around us thought we were too strict, too controlling. Many of them said that one day, our kids would snap and go wild. That we held them to an impossible standard.

But years later, I also remember getting a letter from Jeremiah in the Marine Corps. I remember him writing about how many Marines came to the Corps as Christians and have since turned away from Christ.

But that's not me, Dad, he wrote, *Psalm 1:1, "Blessed is the man that walks not in the counsel of the ungodly, nor stand in the way of sinners, nor sit in the seat of the scornful."*

With tears in my eyes, I can look back and remember. And I can't fully explain how grateful I am that we gave our boys such a solid foundation of faith, even when it was hard. As parents, we never stopped believing in God's promises. We clung to what God said about children who are raised with a strong faith foundation that fall away from faith. He promised that they would always come back, and we clung to that during the times we thought their mistakes would end them.

No, they always returned. And today, their strong foundation has led them to minister to others wherever they go. Because for them, church is not just inside a building on Sundays. It is the world. The Lord called them to minister wherever they go, and I'm proud to say they are doing just that.

That is the Lord's call for you too. To make you a servant of the gospel, sharing its life-saving news with the world. My own past is certainly not perfect, and neither is my children's. Neither was Paul's. But you can use your imperfect past as an advantage to minister to others.

Day 27: Freedom In Chains

An Ad in the Newspaper

After Paul's passionate and clear testimony, Agrippa was stunned. He even said, "In a short time, would you persuade me to be a Christian?" (Acts 26:28).

These words make me wonder if Agrippa was as close as possible to making a decision of faith. Could it be that Paul was about to find favor in the eyes of Agrippa? Is it possible Agrippa *almost* came to believe in Christ?

Sadly, even if that were to be true, *almost* isn't enough. You can't *almost* get forgiven for your sins. *Almost* enter the kingdom of heaven. *Almost* spend eternity with Jesus forever. *Almost* doesn't cut it. And even with Paul's compelling argument, Agrippa still couldn't commit to Jesus. It could be because he was in the company of non-Christian and sinful friends like Bernice, who, if Agrippa became a Christian, could no longer be her friend. It could be because he didn't want to be in chains like Paul was. But it also could be that he was afraid of being called crazy like Festus said to Paul.

After Festus heard Paul talk about Jesus' death, burial, and resurrection, he tells Paul he is out of his mind (v. 24). I mean, it had to have been quite odd seeing a man giddy as can be while on trial and in chains. It does sound a bit crazy for someone to prefer to be imprisoned than *not* share the gospel.

But as Paul wrote in 1 Corinthians 1:18, "For the word of the cross is folly to those who are perishing, but to us who are being saved it is the power of God."

In response to Festus' accusation, Paul answered with kindness rather than judgment. "I am not out of my mind, most excellent Festus" (v. 25). He continued to exhibit love to his enemies and backed up his writings on love in 1 Corinthians 13.

He knew that the will of the father in bad times was more important than the will of people in good times. If that meant he

The Revenant

would remain in chains, all glory to God. That is how much Paul believed in the saving power of the gospel, in the redeeming work of Jesus, in life everlasting.

I heard about a short story that Ernest Hemingway wrote in 1936 called *The Capital of the World.* It's about a young man named Paco who had been kicked out of his house for his misconduct. He wandered the streets of Spain with nowhere to go. Later, when the father missed his son too much to let him go, he took out a local ad in the newspaper. It read, "Paco, meet me at the Hotel Montana at noon on Tuesday. All is forgiven!" When Tuesday rolled around, eight hundred men named Paco came to the hotel to be forgiven.

That many people knew they had done wrong and desired forgiveness. This story paints such a beautiful parallel to the way our sin separates us from God and the way he brings us back in with open arms. It's as though God took out an ad in the local newspaper to get us back. He would do anything to find us when we were lost. To bring him back to himself.

Paul wanted this more than anything for Agrippa and the other Jews. He desired nothing more than to lead nonbelievers to freedom in Christ. But Agrippa wasn't able to accept the forgiveness of sin that Paul shared about. Though Paul offered an opportunity for Agrippa to decide, he ultimately chose to be separated from God.

And Paul? Though he was not guilty, he remained in chains since he appealed to Caesar. His freedom was not granted. But as he made known to everyone, a life in chains in the will of God is better than a life of freedom without Him.

Although in chains, he was freer than anyone there. It was then, it is today, it will be tomorrow. We only have to respond to the ad in the newspaper.

Drop the Anchor

Day 28

"A smooth sea never made a skilled mariner."
English Proverb

"[A]nd he said, 'Do not be afraid, Paul; you must stand before Caesar. And behold, God has granted you all those who sail with you.' So take heart, men, for I have faith in God that it will be exactly as I have been told."

Acts 27:24-25

Did you know out of all the chapters of the Bible, skilled mariners still study Acts 27 today? They use the detailed description of the land and sea to know how to sail their ships. Paul's intricate details give him legitimacy in his experience as a traveler on the Mediterranean. This chapter is all about a shipwreck. One that Paul predicted, and one that none of the other people on the boat were willing to believe. That is, until it was too late.

The Revenant

You see, as Paul was on his way to Rome to see Caesar, the centurion in charge of the ship's direction trusted more in the chief sailor than Paul's opinion. But by this point, Paul had already been shipwrecked three times (2 Corinthians 11:25). He had the experience and perhaps supernatural wisdom to know that it was too dangerous to go on.

The ship was hugging the coast and carried wheat from Egypt to Rome. The sturdy vessel was 180 feet long, 50 feet wide, and 44 feet deep, but it was not seaworthy. There was only one mast, which made movement slow and difficult with wind. There was no steering mechanism, so instead it used large oars to steer the ship, which was incredibly laborious. As you can imagine, rowing and sailing with this large of a ship presented numerous problems to the passengers.

Problematic buzzwords —*difficulty, fear, worry*—appear all over this chapter.

But perhaps the biggest problem was that no one was respecting God's sovereignty. No one even remotely regarded Paul's wise guidance about sailing. Paul deeply believed God because He said they were going to be okay. He told them that Paul was going to meet with Caesar. That's why Paul carried an overwhelming peace that seemed odd in a place of pure panic.

When thinking about Paul being the lone believer in God's promises in the company of doubt, I am reminded of a quote by C. S. Lewis: "When the whole world is running toward a cliff, he who is running in the opposite direction appears to have lost his mind."

All of the passengers on the ship assumed Paul had lost his mind.

I don't think the church today is much different than all those passengers who were ready to "run off the cliff" so to speak. In megachurches across America, how many of them are more focused on distractions like a coffee shop in the lobby, a children's area that resembles Fantasyland at Disney World, a professional light show, a pastor dressed better than Fabio, professionally paid musicians who spend more time gigging in the bar than submerging themselves in God's Word? And how many of the surrounding smaller churches feel pressured to "run off the cliff" to keep up with these larger churches?

Amid problems, doubt, and temptation within the church, God calls us to drop our anchor deeply in Him.

Storms of Life

When you think back on some of the most formative years of your life, what situations or events come to mind? Perhaps it's a time when you stepped out of your comfort zone and moved to a new location. Maybe it was the death of a loved one or a divorce or breakup. It could have been a time in life when you were sick.

Whatever the time, if I had to guess, I imagine that the most formative moment was one that seemed problematic at the time. Like Job says, "man is born to trouble as the sparks fly upward" (Job 5:6-7). Very rarely do churches, businesses, or people grow without hardship.

It's probably why Paul wasn't shaken when the storm started to rage. While on his journey spreading the gospel, problem after problem rose against him. But God continued to prove his faithfulness. Through problems, Paul learned that if God called him to a mission, nothing would stop it from happening. But once the storm started to escalate, the people on the ship began to scramble. Terrified, they let down the dinghy to turn back and sail away. Their problems seemed too big, too terrifying, too hopeless. In their eyes, the only solution was to run away.

The Revenant

But Paul was successful in convincing the people to trust God and wait to sail until morning. "Fearing that we might run on the rocks, they let down four anchors from the stern and prayed for day to come" (Acts 27:29). They dropped the anchor and allowed the Lord to rest on them in the middle of their hardship.

Pastor of Village Church, Matt Chandler, knows firsthand how hardships are a part of growing and a part of the Christian life. One day when reaching down to pick up his child, Matt suddenly passed out and woke up in a hospital. It turns out he had a fast-growing brain tumor. With this heartbreaking news, Matt decided he would preach the gospel through chemo.

He shared that every six months he had to go to the city and sit in the doctor's office. The unfriendly white walls greeted him as the dull music played through the speakers. After waiting in that uncomfortable room, it would be time for the scan. Laying down in the coffin-like CT scan, the panic started to set in as the machine moved and beeped. All he could hear was the ticking of the scanner that was checking for cancer in his body. Afterward, Matt and his wife would shop around the city while they waited for the doctor's news—either the news he wanted to hear or the news he was terrified to hear. Yes, he hated every part of the scan. But you know what else he believed? How much he needed the scan in his life. In the same way, we go through spiritual scans to strengthen our hearts.

Spiritual scans come in the form of hardships. God allows hard times so that we can see how we depend on Him. And when it's all too much to bear, the Lord lifts us up and says He will bear it for us.

When you're struggling to make it out of the house because of some terrible news about a loved one, the Lord says that you can rest on Him. When you're too weary to go to church after your divorce because walking through the doors alone is too much to bear, God says he will carry your weight. When your everyday obligations drain every bit of your time and energy, the Lord says that He will quench your thirst and replenish you.

As Christians, we can look at those potential problems and bring them to the Lord. He wants to help us with the hardships in our lives that so easily trip us up. Sometimes, His help might come in the form of a storm. Why? Because storms make us stronger.

This idea of storms bringing strength is addressed in a different metaphor in the book of Jeremiah. "Moab has been at ease from his youth and has settled on his dregs; he has not been emptied from vessel to vessel, nor has he gone into exile; so his taste remains in him, and his scent is not changed" (Jeremiah 48:11). Some people think the concept here involves wine in a barrel. When they poured wine in a barrel, the sludge ("dregs") goes to the bottom and the wine loses its taste. So, they keep sloshing it into other barrels to make it taste better.

For us to keep our taste, that is our firmness in the Holy Spirit, we need to go through a sloshing process just like wine. We need our taste to come back to life to live out the true meaning of the gospel. In our lives, if we live sludgy, dreadful lives, there's a good chance God will rock us with a storm to bring back taste to the surface again.

Getting Back to the Basics

Last year, I was speaking at a large conference in Downtown Chicago. I met a family there who lives in my town of Bluffton, South Carolina, and connected with the father, Dan. He told me that he attends a small church close by.

"The pastor of our church is amazing," he said, "We've been going there for five years now and we're trying to be an encouragement to him. His young son has cancer and has been

The Revenant

going through a challenging time but is still serving the Lord faithfully." After talking for a few more minutes, I invited him to come visit our church in Bluffton if he ever had a free Sunday, and that was that.

A few months later, I got a call from out of the blue. It was Dan. He abruptly said that he wanted to join our church. He went on to tell me about how the pastor of his small Baptist church was under attack. The session was forcing him to resign because he preached a sermon called, "Are you woke enough yet?" His message addressed topics like transgenderism and how our culture is moving further and further away from God's Word. Attendees started leaving one by one, and the church decided to blame it on the pastor.

As Dan kept rattling off the list of things that the deacons were holding against him, I was stunned. During COVID-19, the pastor got a loan in his name and one for the church. The church loan was forgiven by the government, and the personal loan was paid back with his own finances. But the elder board, rather than doing a full investigation to find the truth tried to dig up negativity about the pastor, tried to make it look like he stole money. They made up lies about him and even started making him feel bad for taking time to see his sick child with cancer. As with most of these circumstances, the entire congregation knew about all of the so-called offenses before bringing them to the pastor.

Toward the end of the conversation, Dan asked me to sit in on a meeting with the deacons of this church. To be honest, I didn't feel comfortable with that since I wasn't involved, but I reluctantly agreed to be there for Dan. But boy, I was not prepared for the yelling, screaming, and blaming that took place in that meeting. The deacons of this church were irate. One woman in attendance spoke up and said that she was saved a month and a

Day 28: Drop The Anchor

half ago when the pastor spoke the Word. She explained that no one reached out to her after that, making her decide she didn't even want to attend the church anymore.

When I heard this, my heart just dropped. How could the church, the very place that should be a place of comfort, acceptance, and peace—be the same place a newly saved person feels like she doesn't belong?

After the meeting, I couldn't help but notice that nobody went up to her to comfort or even address her comments. So I walked toward her and held her hand to remind her that this had nothing to do with God. I told her to keep her eyes on Jesus and not the ones who claim to follow Him.

Once again, C. S. Lewis's words proved true. Both the congregation and the church staff were running toward a cliff, unfazed by the harrowing problems to come. And then there's the pastor running in the opposite direction, appearing to be seemingly crazy, only to end up being the only safe one. Sometimes, following God means looking crazy. It means feeling lonely. To be a Christian is to be different from the world. And God calls us to embrace this exceptionality and use it to point people to Him.

The church was never meant to be a place filled with administrative work, corporate jargon, and business-like management. All too often these things take priority and drive decisions in the church. When that happens it forces the fundamentals of the church to deteriorate. I tried to help rebuild this church as I did with New Life. I offered to disciple them and take them through the sloshing process to get their taste back again. But they denied every offer, just like Moab.

Paul and the ancient church remind us of what the modern-day church so desperately needs to remember. Today's church must work to prioritize the fundamentals—doing life together outside the walls of the church building, embracing the fullness of the gospel in a world determined to drive away from it, breaking bread together, and so much more. None of these basics involve getting sidetracked on money, denominational nuances, or entertainment. The heart of the church is about people and people being loved. Why? Because God showed us through the sacrifice of his son that people are worthy of his love. And without getting back to the basics of the ancient church, this love is impossible to share with others.

As I was researching this chapter, I came across some historic artifacts that were worth bringing up here. In Acts 27, Paul talked about four anchors that were dropped in about fifteen fathoms of water (Acts 27:29). It so happens that four anchors were discovered in Malta and are now on display at the Malta Maritime Museum. They were all discovered in about ninety feet of water, which is exactly fifteen fathoms as is mentioned in Acts 27. All I could think of as I was reflecting on the truth of this passage was *if those anchors could tell a story, what would they say?*

Would they tell of the intense shipwreck that Paul faced that could have prevented him from spreading the good news to the ends of the earth? Would they share about the problems of the ancient church and how it takes a heart of tenacity and commitment to live a life for the gospel?

I wonder about that often.

But if there's one thing I ponder the most about those four anchors, it's the fact that someone had to drop them in the first place. Someone had to make the hard decision—the brave decision—to stop and rest in the middle of hardship. That couldn't have been the easy thing to do. But to live a life with a heart after the gospel requires dropping the anchor. It requires sinking your spirit, actions, and daily routines on Christ's foundation. After all, God sent Jesus from heaven to be our foundation. The church is His holy bride. He bought her with His blood.

All we must do is drop the anchor. Hold steadfast to His Word. Follow the Lord's teaching. His way might not always be the most popular, and it may involve more than one not-so-sunny day.

But when that storm clears and the anchor is lifted, it's time to set sail again. A little different. A little wiser. A little stronger.

No Scar?

Day 29

"Paul's prison became the fulcrum from which he moved the world."

James Stocker

"He lived there two whole years at his own expense, and welcomed all who came to him, proclaiming the kingdom of God and teaching about the Lord Jesus Christ with all boldness and without hindrance."

Acts 28:30-31

At the beginning of this journey together, we set out to rediscover the early church by walking through the book of Acts. It's hard to believe we are coming to the end of our journey. Without a doubt, Paul's long and intense mission for Jesus as told by Luke in this book has opened my eyes to what has been lost in the church today. And what has been lost is exactly what we've been praying that we, the modern church, can bring back to life with the help of the Holy Spirit.

Day 29: No Scar?

The Revenant. The return of someone or something from the dead.

When you began this book, perhaps you were at the same place as me: heartbroken by what the church has become, frustrated at the complacency of Christians, and desperate for a way to bring the church back to life. Maybe your own heart for the Lord needed resurrecting too.

While we dive into Paul's final days of his journey. I invite you to ponder this last chapter with a question in your mind: Do you have any scars?

No Wound, No Scar

Amy Carmichael was an Irish missionary during the 1920s and 1930s. She served the abused and the poor from Belfast to India, where she endured many trials. During her missions, she wrote a poem called "No Scar?". When I read it, I couldn't help but think about Paul's missions. It sounds as though Paul himself could have written it.

No Scar?

Hast thou no scar?
No hidden scar on foot, or side, or hand?
I hear thee sung as mighty in the land,
I hear them hail thy bright ascendant star,
Hast thou no scar?

Hast thou no wound?
Yet I was wounded by the archers, spent,
Leaned Me against a tree to die, and rent
by ravening beasts that compassed Me, I swooned:
Hast thou no wound?

The Revenant

No wound, no scar?
Yet as the Master shall the servant be,
And, pierced are the feet that follow Me;
But thine are whole: can he have followed far
Who has no wound nor scar?

Scars form when deep layers of the skin get damaged. Invisible scars form when the wounds are more psychological and emotional. I think it is safe to say that Paul acquired both types of scars during his missions. Despite every trauma, nothing stopped him from spreading the gospel.

When the crew arrived in Malta, Paul began gathering sticks for a fire to warm around three hundred cold, wet souls. Of all people, *Paul*, the one who was confronted by an angel, was gathering brushwood to kindle the fire. *Paul*. Paul, the great leader who had every right to let other people kindle the fire. But Paul wasn't that kind of leader. To Paul, there was no job too small for a true leader of God. Jesus was an example of this as he washed the disciples' feet and said that he didn't come to be served but to serve (Mark 10:45). Whatever needed to be done, Paul was willing to do it.

While kindling the fire, the heat suddenly brought out a vicious viper. It quickly fastened to Paul's hand, undoubtedly creating yet another scar (Acts 28:3). When the people saw this, they immediately assumed Paul was some kind of terrible murderer. In that region, the people believed when something bad happened to you it was because of a terrible sin. But Paul, confident in his God, flicked the viper off, fulfilling the prophecy by Jesus when he said, "The seventy-two returned with joy, saying, 'Lord, even the demons are subject to us in your name!' And he said to them, 'I saw Satan fall like lightning from heaven. Behold, I have given you authority to tread on serpents and scorpions, and over all the power of the enemy, and nothing shall hurt you' "(Luke 10:17-19).

Day 29: No Scar?

The people were surely waiting for Paul to die. You see, the people knew their snakes and their island, but they did not know Paul's God. Paul had no fear when the viper bit him because he knew the promise of Jesus. He was willing to be scarred by the viper if it meant healing for others. Interestingly enough, history shows us that vipers no longer exist on the island of Malta. Maybe the people developed fearless hearts for dealing with vipers. Maybe Paul started a movement with a fearless approach to life and finally fought the vipers away. God's Word always remains faithful.

After three months, Paul set sail from Malta to Rome with two figureheads on the front of the boat. They were the heads of Caster and Pollux, the twin sons of Zeus. The patron idols of the ancient world were thought to protect sailors while they sailed, which is why they were affixed on the front of the ship. They stayed in Syracuse for three days. Then they sailed to Rhegium, and to Puteoli, where they stayed with some brothers for seven days before making their way to Rome.

You see, Paul longed to return to Rome. Why? Because light always shines the brightest in the darkest of places, and historian Seneca said that Rome was a cesspool of iniquity. You've heard it said that all roads lead to Rome. If that's true, then all roads also lead *from* Rome. That's why Paul wanted to share the gospel in Rome - because it would spread to the rest of the world. We have the gospel in the United States today because of how Paul spread it in Rome!

The Start of an Era

When Paul arrived in Rome, he was allowed to stay by himself with a soldier who guarded him. At the time, two million people lived in Rome—half of them were Roman citizens and half were slaves. Imagine the opportunity for Paul to share the gospel with anyone who had ears to hear. He was also given access to the top leadership in Rome, where some were persuaded by his words and some remained in disbelief. Still in chains, Paul kept on sharing. He never once felt the chains prevented him from spreading God's good news. This ambassador in chains was bound for the hope of Israel.

While he couldn't move freely, Paul was able to move the hearts of the people which goes way further than his feet could take him. Today, we are not chained to our homes. We can take the gospel to our neighborhoods, our schools, and our workplaces. Some will reject the gospel and some will respond. Our only role is to rejoice in the ones who accept it and pray for those who do not.

Paul knew this. He learned from Jesus in the parable of the sower (Matthew 13:1-9) that a fourth of the people who hear the gospel will reject it, with the seed falling on hard soil so the birds can snatch it up immediately. Jesus said that others will respond but only emotionally, so when trials of life come, they fall away. He went on to say that some of the people truly hear and receive the gospel seed. While *some* may accept it, *not all* will bear fruit. Paul told this harsh truth to the people in Rome, but he still received everyone who came to him.

English Evangelist F. B. Meyer wrote that at times, Paul's room would be filled with people, and when they left, the guards would sit beside him and ask questions. At night, soldiers would listen to Paul's testimony and hear of how the Savior was crucified. I imagine they were probably fighting over shifts so they could sit and listen to Paul's stories. Because of Paul's testimony, all of Caesar's household heard the gospel and some received it.

These were the last four years of Paul's life. Four years of endlessly sharing God's word in chains to all who would listen. Scars and all.

Day 29: No Scar?

And you know what? This was the longest period of Paul's incarceration, yet it was also the greatest impact made for the gospel of Christ. God's assignment was Paul's confinement. His suffering and captivity and scars were *all* for the good of those who would receive God's message and be blessed.

Think about it. We watched Paul as he consented to the death of Stephen. We watched him on the way to Damascus when he was blinded and met the Messiah for the first time, only to begin preaching the gospel immediately. We followed him when he was discipled for three years in Arabia in preparation for what God called him to accomplish. To get to Jerusalem, the disciples lowered Paul out of a window and over a wall in Damascus. He stirred up so much trouble in Jerusalem that the disciples shipped him back to Tarsus where Barnabas found him and brought him back to Antioch. From there, Paul made three consecutive journeys around the known Roman world on behalf of Jesus.

And now, here we are in chapter 28.

But what happened to Paul?

The ending is abrupt. In fact, the book ends so oddly that many scholars believe a chapter is missing, but that's not the case.

Later early church writers—Clement and Eusebius from Caesarea—wrote that Paul was released from prison and made his way to Colossi to meet with Philemon. From there, he traveled to Crete where he told Titus to raise up elders in every city to bring stability to the church. After that, it is more than likely that Paul went up the coast to see Timothy one last time, then to Troas where he had the vision of the man from Macedonia calling for help. In Troas, Paul was arrested again and returned to Rome to stand trial before Nero.

Ultimately, Paul lost his head for the gospel.

The Revenant

The end of an era.

Or is it?

Is it possible that the end of Acts is not truly an ending but the *start* of an entirely new era? Ours. Through this book, God calls us to carry on Paul's story to the next generation. God is still acting on behalf of His kingdom and His children. We aren't just readers of a history book; we *are* chapters 29, 30, 31, and so on. We are the modern-day church, the carriers of the beautiful gospel. Because of Paul's dedication and suffering for Christ, we know the Messiah!

About a decade ago, a famous rabbi named Yitzhak Kaduri died in Jerusalem. He passed away at the ripe age of 108 with two hundred thousand people attending his funeral. Before he died, he claimed he knew the identity of the Messiah but would not tell anyone. He wrote the name on a note and gave it to a trusted friend with instructions to open it after his death. In April 2007, his beloved disciples opened the note. To their surprise, the note said, "Yeshua is the Messiah. Many have known His name but have not believed."

I share this story only because two thousand years ago a well-esteemed Pharisee named Saul discovered this same truth, only he didn't keep it hidden. He shared it to the point of death.

Ever since God called Paul to a life of service to the gospel on the road to Damascus, he collected scars of persecution proudly. No scar, no wound, no obstacle ever stopped him from sharing God's good news to the world. His scars told the story of his commitment to the Lord and to the things of the kingdom.

So I ask again *Do you have any scars?* And if you do, what stories do they tell? Every visible and invisible scar should remind you of the resilience God gave you to live for Him in this broken world. They are the roadmap to your healing, a sign of God's strength in you.

Day 29: No Scar?

No wound, no scar.

As we start this new era together with arms linked and hearts on fire for Christ, I want to encourage you with Paul's final words on earth, the words he proclaimed before leaving the Imperial City and entering the Eternal City. May his words awaken the Revenant in you:

> "For I am already being poured out as a drink offering, and the time of my departure has come. I have fought the good fight, I have finished the race, I have kept the faith. Henceforth there is laid up for me the crown of righteousness, which the Lord, the righteous judge, will award to me on that day, and not only to me but also to all who have loved his appearing." (2 Timothy 4:6-8)

Angels in the Cracks

Final Thoughts

Day 30

"I saw the angel in the marble and carved until I set him free."
Michealangelo

We've reached the final day of our journey studying the book of Acts, and somehow our journey is *not* ending. After thirty days of reflecting on the ancient church, it's time to live out the next chapters of Acts. It's our time to wake up the modern church and exemplify what the ancient church did so well.

Paul lived out the gospel to a T. He brought it to the world and everywhere he went, no matter the cost. And God's favor went before him to the end. It's time we revive the way our modern churches operate, so like Paul we can see the miracles and revivals God can bring today.

Day 30: Angels In The Cracks

I just heard about one of these modern miracles from a friend the other day. Every Monday I play golf with some men who have kindly accepted me into their community. They are a fun group of retired men who share the Catholic faith and enjoy golfing together. One of the men, Steve, knows I'm a pastor. He recently went through a serious surgery, and before going into the operation, I called him and prayed with him and his wife. As we walked off the ninth green, Steve thanked me for my prayers and explained that the surgery went well.

"But would you like to hear a story of a miracle that happened recently?" Steve asked.

The truth was that I loved to hear about miracles. I believe they happen daily if we are ready to receive them. "Absolutely," I responded.

Steve went on to tell a story about a friend who lives in the golf community where we were playing. Just the other evening, the friend and his wife were walking their dog when out of nowhere, the friend collapsed and had a massive heart attack in the middle of the road. He was unresponsive, and his wife was unable to find a heartbeat. No one had their phones, so his wife took off running to the crossroads where the traffic was and flagged down the first car she saw. She explained what was happening, and by some incredible miracle, the man driving happened to be an EMS specialist who was off that day. He had everything in his car to revive the man and save his life. By the grace of God, this man happened to be trained in reviving people from heart attacks and stabilize their vitals, which was why he had the equipment in his car.

It was not a coincidence or luck or chance. This is a miracle, one that God still does today. This story *is* Acts chapter 29, 30, 31, and so on. As we continue to revive the modern church, God has new miracles for each believer going hard after the gospel

The Revenant

as we embrace our spiritual gifts. What is true is that while many people in the modern church are walking away from spiritual gifts, the Lord has never stopped using them in His believers. The miracles and healing in Acts were not only for that time. Even throughout the New Testament, there was no place where those gifts came to an end. That's because there is no limit to what God can do—and is there anything more exciting than that?

My son Isaiah, the junior at Liberty University, recently went to an outdoor revival service. As my wife and I were watching it online, the president of the university announced that he was excited for them to return after summer since the university was going to study the book of Acts together and revisit the early church. When I heard it, I just smiled with a sense of confirmation that the Holy Spirit called me to write *The Revenant*, to bring believers back to where we began. To let people who feel they are too flawed to be used can remember their value and potential. To let people who have never truly followed Jesus know they can live out a biblical outline and see something beautiful come from their life. To offer megachurches a tool to rediscover their roots and create small life groups to shape their community. To remind smaller churches they are more valuable and impactful than they will ever know.

The Revenant is about looking back while simultaneously moving forward. When we take what we learn from looking at the ancient church, we can move forward with hope and knowledge in spreading the gospel successfully.

No matter where you are in your journey, remember that *The Revenant* is about bringing what is dead back to life. During the Renaissance, some of the greatest artists, musicians, and sculptors were competing to get their work into the Italian cathedral. The famous sculptor Michelangelo is most known for

Day 30: Angels In The Cracks

sculpting the statue of King David during this period. But what some do not know is how he accomplished that artistic feat.

All the other sculptors during that time would only accept perfect pieces of marble so they could create a sculpture so perfect that it could be presented to the cathedral without flaw. But Michelangelo thought differently. He used a piece of cracked marble that everyone else rejected to begin his sculpture. With this cracked marble, he created the sculpture of King David. Of course, people asked why he used the imperfect marble. He famously said, "I saw the angel in the marble and carved until I set him free."

It's no secret that the church has its own cracks and flaws like that piece of marble. It did in ancient times, and it does now. But those cracks do not define the church. Why? Because we're all cracked. And God accepts us with open arms to make us into something priceless.

Michelangelo was able to see the angel through the cracks. He wasn't afraid to embrace the imperfect marble, because he knew he could create something wonderful out of it. That's how he was able to create a sculpture so acclaimed that viewers have flocked to Europe to view it for over five hundred years.

Revival can come with cracks, scars, bruises, and failures. Life can be given to any who asks our Lord for it. We just have to trust that there are angels in the cracks. God bless you on your journey in the revenant life.

Thank you so much for reading The Revenant. When God uses you to move the gospel and works miracles in your life, please share your stories with me by going to christianchapman.org.